Whitman College
Walla Walla, Washington

*Written by Carly Sanders
Edited by Kevin Nash*

*Additional contributions by Omid Gohari,
Christina Koshzow, Chris Mason, Joey Rahimi,
Jon Skindzier, Luke Skurman, Tim Williams,
Adam Burns and Sara Ginsberg*

COLLEGE PROWLER

ISBN # 1-59658-204-9
ISSN # 1552-1842
© Copyright 2005 CollegeProwler
All Rights Reserved
Printed in the U.S.A.
www.collegeprowler.com

Special thanks to Babs Carryer, Andy Hannah, LaunchCyte, Tim O'Brien, Bob Sehlinger, Thomas Emerson, Andrew Skurman, Barbara Skurman, Bert Mann, Dave Lehman, Daniel Fayock, Chris Babyak, The Donald H. Jones Center for Entrepreneurship, Terry Slease, Jerry McGinnis, Bill Ecenberger, Idie McGinty, Kyle Russell, Jacque Zaremba, Larry Winderbaum, Paul Kelly, Roland Allen, Jon Reider, Team Evankovich, Julie Fenstermaker, Lauren Varacalli, Abu Noaman, Jason Putorti, Mark Exler, Daniel Steinmeyer, Jared Cohon, Gabriela Oates, Tri Ad Litho, David Koegler, Glen Meakem, and **the Whitman College Bounce Back Team.**

CollegeProwler™
5001 Baum Blvd.
Suite 456
Pittsburgh, PA 15213

Phone: (412) 697-1390, 1(800) 290-2682
Fax: (412) 697-1396, 1(800) 772-4972
E-mail: info@collegeprowler.com
Website: www.collegeprowler.com

CollegeProwler™ is not sponsored by, affiliated with, or approved by Carnegie Mellon University in any way.

CollegeProwler™ strives to faithfully record its sources. As the reader understands, opinions, impressions, and experiences are necessarily personal and unique. Accordingly, there are, and can be, no guarantees of future satisfaction extended to the reader.

© Copyright 2005 CollegeProwler. All rights reserved. No part of this work may be reproduced or transmitted in any form or by any means, including but not limited to, photocopy, recording, or any information storage and retrieval systems, without the express written permission of CollegeProwler™.

Welcome to College Prowler™

During the writing of College Prowler's guidebooks, we felt it was critical that our content was unbiased and unaffiliated with any college or university. We think it's important that our readers get honest information and a realistic impression of the student opinions on any campus — that's why if any aspect of a particular school is terrible, we (unlike a campus brochure) intend to publish it. While we do keep an eye out for the occasional extremist — the cheerleader or the cynic — we take pride in letting the students tell it like it is. We strive to create a book that's as representative as possible of each particular campus. Our books cover both the good and the bad, and whether the survey responses point to recurring trends or a variation in opinion, these sentiments are directly and proportionally expressed through our guides.

College Prowler guidebooks are in the hands of students throughout the entire process of their creation. Because you can't make student-written guides without the students, we have students at each campus who help write, randomly survey their peers, edit, layout, and perform accuracy checks on every book that we publish. From the very beginning, student writers gather the most up-to-date stats, facts, and inside information on their colleges. They fill each section with student quotes and summarize the findings in editorial reviews. In addition, each school receives a collection of letter grades (A through F) that reflect student opinion and help to represent contentment, prominence, or satisfaction for each of our 20 specific categories. Just as in grade school, the higher the mark the more content, more prominent, or more satisfied the students are with the particular category.

Once a book is written, additional students serve as editors and check for accuracy even more extensively. Our bounce-back team — a group of randomly selected students who have no involvement with the project — are asked to read over the material in order to help ensure that the book accurately expresses every aspect of the university and its students. This same process is applied to the 200-plus schools College Prowler currently covers. Each book is the result of endless student contributions, hundreds of pages of research and writing, and countless hours of hard work. All of this has led to the creation of a student information network that stretches across the nation to every school that we cover. It's no easy accomplishment, but it's the reason that our guides are such a great resource.

When reading our books and looking at our grades, keep in mind that every college is different and that the students who make up each school are not uniform — as a result, it is important to assess schools on a case-by-case basis. Because it's impossible to summarize an entire school with a single number or description, each book provides a dialogue, not a decision, that's made up of 20 different topics and hundreds of student quotes. In the end, we hope that this guide will serve as a valuable tool in your college selection process. Enjoy!

OMID GOHARI ○ CHRISTINA KOSHZOW ○ CHRIS MASON ○ JOEY RAHIMI ○ LUKE SKURMAN ○
The College Prowler™ Team

WHITMAN COLLEGE
Table of Contents

By the Numbers............................ **1**	Drug Scene................................ **85**
Academics **4**	Campus Strictness **89**
Local Atmosphere **9**	Parking.. **93**
Safety and Security.................... **14**	Transportation **97**
Computers.................................. **20**	Weather.................................... **103**
Facilities..................................... **25**	Report Card Summary **107**
Campus Dining.......................... **30**	Overall Experience **108**
Off-Campus Dining **35**	The Inside Scoop..................... **112**
Campus Housing **41**	Finding a Job or Internship **117**
Off-Campus Housing................. **50**	Alumni Information................. **119**
Diversity..................................... **54**	Student Organizations............ **121**
Guys and Girls **59**	The Best & Worst..................... **123**
Athletics..................................... **67**	Visiting Campus....................... **125**
Nightlife..................................... **74**	Words to Know........................ **130**
Greek Life **80**	

Introduction from the Author

Growing through my adolescent years on a small, secluded, rural island in Washington state, I viewed college as an opportunity to escape and venture as far away from home as possible and abandon everything familiar. Isn't that what college is about? So when my parents suggested I apply to Whitman, I thought, "Yeah, right…like I'm gonna put out all that effort in applying to schools and taking these damn standardized tests just to go to Whitman in the same state!" Little did I know.

As it turned out, Whitman was the first school I got into and the last school I ever expected I'd end up at. After all, it's in Walla Walla—the home of wheat fields, the state penitentiary, pseudo-hicks, farm country, and good wine (if I was of age, I could actually drink it). But when I really sat down and thought about what makes me happy, what makes me truly happy in my education, Whitman fit everything I knew I wanted at that time: a place where excellence is expected academically and in lifestyle, but not without a sense of humor or at the expense of a social life; a place where professors genuinely care about students and their interests, but without pounding on professors' office doors waiting in line for your ten minutes of one-on-one time; a place where students are accepting of diverse and quirky interests, but not criticizing or judgmental; and perhaps, more important than all of these aspects, a place where the people make the school, where students are comfortable enough to be themselves, and be friendly and just plain happy, where students feel special and motivated by their own impulse and know they have something to contribute and that they should.

Though Whitman has been a great place for myself and most of the students I've talked to, it certainly doesn't fit everyone. Ultimately, my hope is that you, a prospective college student, will not merely consider the exterior glamour of statistics and colorful brochures of schools you research on your quest for "the perfect school." Here's a news flash: The "perfect school" doesn't exist! What is possible and, perhaps, more important is to look inside and ask yourself: What makes me happy? What will I need for the next four years of my life, and does this school offer it? Trust your gut; you might end up in the last place you thought you would.

Carly N. Sanders
Whitman College

By the Numbers

General Information
Whitman College
345 Boyer Avenue
Walla Walla, Washington
99362

Control:
Private, 4-year or above

Academic Calendar:
Semester

Religious Affiliation:
None

Founded:
1883

Website:
www.whitman.edu

Main Phone:
(509) 527-5111

Admissions Phone:
(509) 527-5176

Student Body
Full-Time Undergraduates:
1,415

Part-Time Undergraduates:
39

Male Undergraduates:
645 (44%)

Female Undergraduates:
809 (56%)

Admissions

Overall Acceptance Rate:
51%

Early Decision Acceptance Rate:
82%

Regular Acceptance Rate:
49%

Total Applicants:
2,345

Total Acceptances:
1,196

Freshman Enrollment:
362

Yield (percentage of admitted students who actually enroll):
32%

Qualified applicants placed on waiting list:
288

Applicants accepting a place on waiting list:
100

Students enrolled from waiting list:
34

Early Decision Available?
Yes

Early Action Available?
No

Early Decision One Deadline:
November 15

Early Decision One Notification:
December 15

Regular Decision Deadline:
January 15

Regular Decision Notification:
April 1

Must Reply-By Date:
May 1

Common Application Accepted?
Yes

Supplemental Forms?
Yes

Admissions Phone:
(509) 527-5176

Admissions E-mail:
admission@whitman.edu

Admissions Website:
www.whitman/edu/admission

SAT I or ACT Required?
Either

First-Year Students Submitting SAT Scores:
306 (84%)

**SAT I Range
(25th – 75th Percentile):**
1230 - 1430

**SAT I Verbal Range
(25th – 75th Percentile):**
620 - 730

**SAT I Math Range
(25th – 75th Percentile):**
610 - 700

Retention Rate:
95% (returning students after freshman year)

Transfer Applications Received:
74

Transfer Applicants Offered Admission:
43

Transfer Applicants Enrolled:
32

Top 10% of High School Class:
59%

Application Fee:
$45

Financial Information

Tuition:
$27,106

Room and Board:
$7,180

Books and Supplies:
$1,350

Average Need-Based Financial Aid Package:
$17,750

Students Who Applied For Financial Aid:
51%

Students Who Applied For Financial Aid and Received it:
42%

Financial Aid Phone:
(509) 527-5178

Financial Aid E-mail:
finaid@whitman.edu

Financial Aid Website:
www.whitman.edu/financial_aid

Academics

The Lowdown On...
Academics

Degree Awarded
Bachelor's

Most Popular Areas of Study
14% Biology technician/biotechnology laboratory technician
13% Biology/biological sciences
13% Political science and government
8% English language and literature
8% History

Full-time Faculty
116

Faculty with Terminal Degree
82%

Student-to-Faculty Ratio
10:1

Average Course Load
16 credits

Special Degree Options
Double Major
Dual Enrollment
Student Exchange Program
Honors Program
Independent Study
Internships
Liberal Arts Career Combo
Student Designed Major
Study Abroad
Teacher Certification

Best Places to Study
Penrose Library
Maxey Hall

Four-year Graduation Rate:
74%

Five-year Graduation Rate:
84%

Six-year Graduation Rate:
85%

Did You Know?

- Whitman **offers over forty majors** and combined programs.

- Whitman offers 5-year programs affiliated with such schools as **Columbia, The University of Washington, and Duke**.

Students Speak Out On...
Academics

> "**Classes are often enjoyable and unexpected because they constantly force students to look at the world in different ways, and to challenge and consider their own views.**"

"**Professors really want to help you learn,** and they are so passionate about what they teach!"

"**All of my classes have been interesting**, but the best aspect is that professors are very approachable."

"I find my classes very interesting. They encourage me to **apply the ideas I'm learning** to other spheres of academia."

"Professors at Whitman are **very interested in getting to know their students** not simply on an academic level, but on a personal level, as well."

"I've found my professors to be **extremely approachable and open**. Several have become close personal friends, as well. Professors care about developing a relationship with their students."

"Such a relationship allows students to achieve **a more rounded education** because these positive relationships foster increased interest in learning and analytical thinking."

Q "**Professors frequently go out to lunch with students** or invite them to their offices for chats."

Q "Classes at Whitman are demanding, be it a class of two people or of thirty. **Classes require preparation and alertness**."

Q "All of the teachers that I have had **genuinely care about my well-being**, and that has been a real treat."

The College Prowler Take On...
Academics

Experiences can depend, of course, on what classes you take, but most students find classes interesting and engaging, primarily because professors are talented in and love what they teach. Students find a comfortable environment in which to discuss all facets of academia and generally find their professors to be animated in classes and easy to talk to both in and outside of the classroom. Students also find Whitman to be an arena that encourages the exploration of academic diversity. Whitman has loose distribution requirements: the requirements can be fulfilled by a wide range of eclectic classes in order for students to not only explore their interests, but find their focus while doing so. The distribution categories include Social Sciences (minimum of six credits); Humanities (at least six credits); Fine Arts (at least six); Science (also six, and at least one lab credit); Quantitative Analysis (at least three credits which can be filled by several mathematics courses, some psychology and sociology courses, and several science courses, as well); and Alternative Voices (including core, the full-year required course for all first-year students that is based on works that demonstrate the progression of Western thought).

Though it probably depends on your major, the faculty makes a genuine effort to get to know their students and find out what "makes them tick" rather than being just another bland face in a classroom. It's never uncommon for students to go to the homes of professors for dinner gatherings, to watch films for class, or to just socialize with other students in their areas of study—I actually take banjo lessons from my writing professor, free of charge! The ratio of students to faculty is also small (10:1). Professors are also insanely intelligent, too—ninety-eight percent of tenure track faculty has their Ph.D. or an appropriate terminal degree in their field, making classes extremely demanding.

The College Prowler™ Grade on
Academics: A-

A high Academics grade generally indicates that professors are knowledgeable, accessible, and genuinely interested in their students' welfare. Other determining factors include class size, how well professors communicate, and whether or not classes are engaging.

Local Atmosphere

The Lowdown On...
Local Atmosphere

Region:
Pacific Northwest

City, State:
Walla Walla, Washington

Setting:
Small City with Rural and some Suburban qualities

Distance from:
Seattle - 4.5 hours
Spokane - 3 hours

City Websites:
www.wallawalla.org
wcts.whitman.edu/wallawalla

Points of Interest:
Whitman Mission National Historic Site
Local wineries
Pioneer Park
State Penitentiary

Closest Shopping:
Downtown on Main Street, Tri-Cities (45-60-minute drive away)

Closest Movie Theatres:
Grand Cinemas
1390 W. Poplar Street
(1.78 miles, or 5-minute drive from campus)
(509) 527-5222

Did You Know?
Five Fun Facts about Walla Walla:

- "Walla Walla," of Native American origin, means "**many waters**" because of the many streams that ran through the area.
- Walla Walla hosts the festival, "**Woodstick**", which showcases local musicians and artists as well as the "Walla Walla Sweet Onion Blues Fest", which promotes local blues musicians, restaurants, artists, and craftsman.
- Every May, Walla Walla also hosts the annual **Balloon Stampede**, where the fairgrounds are overtaken with hot air balloons for several days.
- Walla Walla has **seventeen public city parks**, and an aviary that encompasses over 600 acres of grass and trees, playgrounds, trails, and pools.
- There are over **thirty-five wineries and over 1,000 acres of vineyards** in the area.

Famous People from Walla Walla:
William O. Douglas '20 - U.S. Supreme Court
Ralph Cordiner '22 - CEO and Chairman, General Electric Corp.
Walter Brattain '24 - Physicist, Nobel Prize Winner
Adam West '51 - Actor, "Batman"
Matt Ames '70 - Director of Research, Mayo Clinic
Ryan Crocker '71 - U.S. Ambassador to Afghanistan
John Stanton '77 - Founder and CEO, Western Wireless & Voice Stream

Local Slang:
Pop – what a native from Walla Walla calls soda
Sketchy – describes something strange or odd

Students Speak Out On...
Local Atmosphere

> "Because the town of Walla Walla is so small, our socializing is quite campus-centric, which translates into some pretty happening events."

Q "**As a geology major, Walla Walla is perfect for what I'm studying**—the terrain is very diverse and the strata layers are clearly visible. The area has some interesting landforms and a rich geological history, so I feel like I lucked out. I didn't grow up in a metropolitan area either, so Walla Walla's mild atmosphere suits me fine."

Q "**The whole area seems to be a place that appreciates music**, which I really like. Local bands often play downtown or local musicians will come to Whitman to see our concerts. It's a really nice exchange to have, especially since it feels like other ties to the Walla Walla community are minimal if not non-existent. There isn't a whole lot of interaction between the locals and the Whitties."

Q "**There's pretty much nothing to do in Walla Walla**, unless you're bored or desperate or both. In a way, it's nice because it brings the focus of activity to Whitman, but it's always really frustrating when I want to leave Whitman for a while and experience some rich culture—and Walla Walla can't offer it."

Q "Since Walla Walla is known for its farming, it is agriculturally based and that greatly affects the atmosphere. **It is not a cosmopolitan town, but there are good places to go out for dinner**. I grew up near a large city, so I definitely miss it, and sometimes feel suffocated by the remoteness of Walla Walla. It helps that the people are nice, but nothing replaces the city."

Q "**There are no other large universities**. I feel the students of Whitman College have all the attention and I like it that way."

Q "**The highlight [of Walla Walla] is the nature**, whether in the parks or out in the wheat fields."

Q "**Visit the wheat fields and the Blue Mountains**! The surrounding area is beautiful!"

Q "**Watching the sunset at the wheat fields is a must**! And Pioneer Park is a fun place for a picnic or an afternoon jog. There's always something to do outdoors here, and when it's sunny, most everyone is, even locals."

Q "Walla Walla has got everything I need: **A coffee shop, grocery store, thrift store, movie theatre, and a couple of nice restaurants**. It's good if you like the simpler life, and it's refreshing to go off campus if I'm stressed, and not be bombarded with all the grittiness or busyness of a city."

Q "Everything here is great. **I don't feel like I'm missing anything**."

Q "Walla Walla is a big dud-city, but it all depends on what you're looking for. **For Walla Walla's size, they offer quite a bit of variety** with a K-Mart, Wal-Mart, several grocery stores, fast food joints, restaurants, video rental places, wineries, and lots of stuff to do outside. Sometimes it gets on my nerves, but I don't go off campus too often anyway, and Whitman has some good stuff going on so I don't need to."

The College Prowler Take On...
Local Atmosphere

In terms of how adequate the local atmosphere is, it definitely depends on what you're looking for and what satisfies you in an environment. Seeing as how Whitman's in Walla Walla—also known as the "boonies" or the "middle of nowhere," it seems that most students say the local atmosphere, for the most part, is pretty quiet and limited, but is also focused on more outdoor activities. There are a few places to go that are entertaining: the movie theater, local bars, and some good restaurants. Walla Walla residents are pretty divided when it comes to how they feel about Whitman College—some say "thank goodness for Whitman for bringing a more liberal perspective," while others feel that the campus creates too much difficulty and noise for the charm and quiet of Walla Walla. The small size of Walla Walla does seem to limit how eclectic the local atmosphere is and how rich of a culture it can offer. Though Walla Walla also has Walla Walla College (a 7th Day Adventist school) and Walla Walla Community College, not much socializing or mixing goes on between these environments and Whitman, though students from these two other schools have been known to attend some of the events Whitman hosts, especially open dances and concerts (for a small fee, usually).

Although Walla Walla is small, it does offer some lovely attractions, especially outdoors with its natural beauty. If you're someone who loves exploring the outdoors and appreciates nature, this school is very ideally located for those interests. Overall, the consensus seems to be this: be prepared for a small-town- feel, and less variety than a metropolitan area, ranging from shopping, to artistic culture, to activities for young people, to clubs and bars.

The College Prowler™ Grade on Local Atmosphere: C+

A high Local Atmosphere grade indicates that the area surrounding campus is safe and scenic. Other factors include nearby attractions, proximity to other schools, and the town's attitude toward students

Safety & Security

The Lowdown On...
Safety & Security

Number of Whitman College Police:
(509) 527-5777 or 7-911 from residence halls / 9-911 from campus buildings (Walla Walla Police Department) for emergencies, (509) 527-4434 or (509) 527-1960 (Walla Walla Police Department) for non-emergencies

Safety Services:
Security Escorts, "Yellow Jacket" Escorts (7:00 pm – 1:00 am), Security Phones ("blue light" phones), bicycle registration

Health Services:
17 infirmary beds, physician available for examination and consultation Monday through Friday 8:00 to 9:30 am (there is no cost for this service for full-time students).

Health Center Office Hours:
24-hours a day, 7 days a week

Did You Know?

- The City of **Walla Walla requires that all bicycles be registered** with the Walla Walla Police Department. Registration costs $5, and has proven to be an effective method for retrieving stolen bicycles, since the owner can be traced and the bike returned if found. During the first two weeks of the academic year, Whitman Security registers any bicycle on campus. After the two-week period, bicycles have to be registered at the Police Station, located in City Hall (on the corner of 3rd and Rose St.).

- All Whitman students are allowed to use the services provided at the Health Center, regardless of their insurance coverage.
- Prescriptions may be filled and delivered to the Health Center from a local pharmacy. Certain prescriptions may be available from the Health Center at a nominal cost. They also stock a few over-the-counter medications for resale. These may all be charged to your student account.
- The Health Center performs some laboratory tests such as strep, mono, urinalysis, and pregnancy tests on-site for a nominal cost.
- Allergy antigens are administered per private MD's orders at a nominal cost. Such injections are available only during regularly scheduled physician hours.
- Crutches are available for loan at no cost. A deposit is charged to your student account and removed when the item is returned.
- The Health Center provides whirlpool and ultrasound treatments for post-injury care.
- The staff assists students in obtaining referrals outside the Health Center to reliable and competent community professionals in the area of specialty requested. (All charges incurred at outside resources are the responsibility of the student.)
- Transportation to outside health resources are provided by previous arrangement. Available Monday through Friday, 8:00 a.m. to 12 noon and 1:00 to 2:30 p.m.

Safety and Security (*Continued...*)

- Physical examinations required by outside facilities (overseas study, Peace Corps, grad schools, etc.) done by appointment and at a nominal cost. Varsity physical exams are coordinated with the Athletic Department.
- Health Center staff offers assistance in obtaining specialized women's health care through various community resources.
- Body Composition Analysis is available at a nominal cost. Individual or group nutritional counseling and weight management programs will be provided as needed and requested.
- The Health Center provides anonymous HIV tests.
- Sexual assault exams can be performed at the Health Center or our staff assists you in obtaining this care at an outside facility if you choose.
- Postcoital contraception (Morning After Treatment) is dispensed at a nominal cost.
- Condoms may be purchased for 10 cents each.

The Health Center Administrative Assistants are happy to assist you with insurance claims processing and benefit coordination.

- There is a study area and resource mini-library available with health education materials.
- There are opportunities for interested students to be involved as health-care aides or through our organized student health group, WISH.
- A variety of health education programs may be arranged for individual groups in campus facilities or in the Health Center.
- A meeting room is available for small health-related groups or meetings.
- The Counseling Center also offers personal and psychological counseling by professionally trained counselors to all students at no charge. Counselors assist individuals and groups with personal and academic concerns, career choices, interpersonal relationships, and other areas of concern or interest.

Students Speak Out On...
Safety & Security

> "Especially with the library being open twenty-four hours, the whole campus is very much a 'round-the-clock' community. Even though the school is small, I always run into someone when I'm walking around, no matter what time."

Q "Though parts of Walla Walla have been known to have their crime, **the Whitman campus overall is very safe**, very good, and amazing. I never feel threatened walking around campus, even at night."

Q |"Security and safety is pretty tight. **They like to keep us safe**."

Q "Campus security is accessible and the nearness of the campus community makes students feel safe. **The surrounding areas are all residential**, so I don't feel like there's any major harm nearby."

Q "I feel very safe around campus, even walking around at night. Especially on the weekends, **there are always people walking around until really late**, and I usually run into friends to meet up with if I'm by myself."

Q "The campus is very safe. As a nineteen year-old girl, I feel safe walking around campus by myself. **Guys are always willing to walk you back** to wherever you need to go, which is really nice too. Generally though, I don't feel like I need anyone to escort me."

Q "**Students are very trusting with each other**. I had more things stolen from me in high school than I did at Whitman. I don't think I've ever locked my door either, which is nice. Theft is not a big issue, although some students have occasionally had bikes stolen or taken for a while. Usually it's just other students who borrowed the bike for a while and didn't give it back yet."

Q "**I definitely feel comfortable leaving the door to my room unlocked**. Most students do, and it's more of a pain when you need to get into your room, and you have to fumble for your keys to unlock it. The outside doors to the dorms are also locked at 9:00 pm, so it doesn't really seem that necessary to lock individual dorm rooms, since that basically keeps all the weirdos out."

Q "**I have never experienced any danger on campus**, even walking home at 3:00 a.m. from the library many nights. If it's during finals, a lot of people are walking home at 3:00 a.m. too, or sometimes later."

Q "I've called the yellow jackets to help out a couple of times, but **I've never actually needed them**. It's just nice to know they're there to help out if I need them. They also come around and check to make sure our doors are locked in the IHC [Interest House Community]."

The College Prowler Take On...
Safety & Security

Since the campus is relatively small, and everything is within walking distance, it's pretty easy for security to monitor such a concentrated area, and most students never feel threatened by outside visitors or other students. Most of the campus is well-lit at night and very visible to others—there really aren't any dark, dreary, sketchy alleys to avoid. Whitman's campus security is also very responsive and prompt, and really cares about the safety and well being of students. Because most students wander around in groups at night, especially during the weekends when parties and events are going on, it is rare for students to not run into other students, and those students walking alone usually join some group to wander with if they desire.

As for theft, though it has happened (especially with bikes—there was an epidemic where a community member stole several unlocked Whitman bikes), most students feel it's not a huge problem. In fact, many students at the library will set-up their study areas with their computers, notes, and books and will leave for a period of time to take a break, be it in the library or not, and return to find their belongings untouched. All-in-all, students feel the environment is very safe and trusting, and since the community of students is tightly-knit where most people know each other, most students don't feel threatened.

A

The College Prowler™ Grade on
Safety & Security: A

A high grade in Safety & Security means that students generally feel safe, campus police are visible, blue-light phones and escort services are readily available, and safety precautions are not overly necessary.

Computers

The Lowdown On...
Computers

High-Speed Network?
Yes

Wireless Network?
Yes

Number of Labs:
5

Number of Computers:
270

Operating Systems:
PC
MAC

Charge to Print?
No

Free Software:
Virus Protection Software (McAfee VirusScan Home Edition for Windows; Virex for Macintoshes). This software must be reinstalled yearly, or it expires.
Various utility programs like Telnet SSH, FTP programs.

24-Hour Labs:
Penrose Library
All other labs with student swipe-card

Did You Know?

- For its size, Whitman has one of the largest ratios of students per computer at any private liberal arts school.

- Students in residence halls can arrange to have an internet connection as fast as 1.5M/256K in their rooms.

- Wireless networking is available in almost all academic buildings, and is soon to be added to popular outdoor areas on campus.

- General access computing facilities in Penrose Library and Maxey Hall are open 24/7.

- Whitman's Penrose Library is open 24/7.

- Students using Penrose Library can check out wireless laptops if they don't already have a laptop of their own.

Discounted Software

While Whitman doesn't have any particular arrangements set up with any software companies, students qualify for student discounts on any piece of software out there that offers such a discount. Some particularly good ones include Microsoft Office programs (either the whole Office suite - Word/Excel/Powerpoint, or just the individual components (just Word, for example). Depending on whether students need a Mac or Windows version, they may be able to get the whole suite for $149 for example (a very good discount off the normal price which is well over $300).

Students Speak Out On...
Computers

> "The labs usually have free spaces, and the library is also full of computers for students to use [though you do have to login and be a Whitman student to use most of them]."

Q "**Computers are always available somewhere**. Whitman keeps us well stocked."

Q "[There are] tons of computers available, particularly for a small school. **It's great to have so much accessibility**, primarily because students depend on computers so much for papers, reports, labs, or e-mail."

Q "**It is nice to have your own computer**, but you are bound to find a computer at any of the computer labs readily available to you at any time."

Q "Most people bring their own computers with them, and more specifically, laptops. But though most people have computers, **many use the computer labs for printing papers**, so get to a lab early if you want to print a paper out before class!"

Q "**Computer labs that are open everyday for twenty-four hours are rarely full**."

Q "Generally in some academic building, **computers are always available somewhere** along with printing capabilities."

Q "**The computer labs are well stocked and staffed**, although near finals they can tend to fill up. In the library and science building students can also borrow laptops."

Q "Especially during hectic times of the year, like mid-terms and finals, library computers are hard to come by. **My recommendation is to work either in Maxey or the Science Building**—there are always computers available there, and the environment is much quieter than the library."

Q "What is nice at the library is that **you can 'check out' laptops for four hours at a time** and work anywhere in the library (they even have wireless Internet). Just make sure to get there early because they go really fast, and it's hard to get one once they're all gone."

Q "**I prefer having my own computer** (hooking up to the network is really easy), but there are so many available computers on campus that it's not necessary."

Q "The campus is fully wired. Dorm rooms and interest houses all have Internet hook-ups and the **academic buildings have wireless networks**."

Q "I brought my own computer with me, but **it really wasn't necessary for school purposes**. If you're really into chatting, gaming, or e-mail, a computer of your own may be more crucial. The Ethernet is a T1, so it's about middle-of-the-road as far as speediness goes."

Q "One can always find an open computer, either in the computer labs or in the library, so a computer is not necessary. The best thing about the computer network is **being able to download so much music**."

The College Prowler Take On...
Computers

Being that academics are a very high priority at Whitman, and being that in today's world it's virtually impossible to not use a computer in academia, Whitman ensures that students have access to computers. Though most students bring their own PCs or laptops to school to have in their rooms, Whitman also provides several computer labs, most of which are accessible at any time of day or night. It is probably more convenient for students to bring their own computers, but there are many labs that are open for most, if not all, of the day. Computer availability varies depending on the time of year, and it's very challenging to find one during finals.

All-in-all, Whitman treats their students very well with providing the proper technological equipment to perform well academically. The Internet is also easily accessible, and most students check their e-mail several times a day (yes, some are a little obsessed, but e-mails are frequently sent around campus too—list serve debates can be highly amusing). Whitman does a good job at providing computers, and most have never encountered any complaints or major difficulties (except occasionally some troubles during finals when the library is overflowing with studying students).

B+

The College Prowler™ Grade on Computers: B+

A high grade in Computers designates that computer labs are available, the computer network is easily accessible, and the campus' computing technology is up-to-date.

Facilities

The Lowdown On...
Facilities

What Is There to Do?
Most students spend their time outdoors in between classes on Ankeny Field playing Frisbee, reading, or chatting when the weather is nice. Otherwise, students go to RCC to check their mail at their student mailboxes or their e-mail, and grab a bite to eat. Many also go to Sherwood Athletic Center or get some kind of exercise as well, and some do last minute reading or preparation for classes.

Campus size:
61 acres

Movie Theater on Campus?
Sadly no, but Hunter Auditorium usually has weekly showings of movies, free of charge for students. Once each semester, the Campus Activities Boars (CAB) shows movies on a huge screen on the side lawn of Reid Campus Center.

Bowling on Campus?
No, but it is a good idea, and one that most students wouldn't be opposed to. There are a couple of bowling allies not too far away from campus—maybe a ten-minute drive at the most.

Bar on Campus?
No, but the Brew Pub is about a two-minute walk from campus, and Rosita's, which serves alcohol (though it's a family Mexican restaurant by day), and is just beyond the Brew Pub a couple of blocks on Main Street.

Coffeehouse on Campus?
Yep, the Reid Campus Center Coffeehouse is located downstairs in the building.

Student Center:
Reid Campus Center (known as RCC).

Athletic Center:
Sherwood Center, soon to be renovated though.

Libraries:
Penrose Library, Career Center Library

Favorite Things to Do:
Whitman is a place where students are always out and about, and they can't get enough of the outdoors. Usually students play Frisbee, and there's actually a "Frisbee Golf" course outlined on the campus where students often gather in groups and play between classes. Students also love intramural sports, and practices are held on Ankeny in the afternoons when classes are finished. Visiting the wheat fields in the evenings to see sunsets is also a popular activity. Almost every weekend there's also a musical event of some kind put on by students (for instance, Coffeehouse has live music almost every Friday night, usually by students).

Popular Places to Chill:
Either Ankeny Field, RCC, or in peoples' respective dorms. Many students also venture downtown to the Starbucks, Merchants, or Coffee Perk, which all offer great places to sit outside. A lot of where students are found depends on the weather in large part—when it's sunny students are hanging out anywhere that the sun is shining.

Students Speak Out On...
Facilities

> "Reid campus center [student center] is the newest building on campus, and it's very nicely designed. There are always people inside chatting or doing something, and I always run into friends there."

- "**Facilities are top notch and always improving**. It seems like the school builds a new building every year and replaces the old, shotty one."

- "**RCC is really remarkable**. It houses many of the most important groups on campus: the newspaper, Bluemoon staff, multi-cultural center, student services and the dean of students, ASWC [Associated Students of Whitman College], meeting rooms, KWCW [radio station], and even a dark room for photography savvy folks."

- "The new science building addition is beautiful, and it was just finished last year. **The decorations inside are also really nice**, and it has a planetarium inside too. It's a great place to hang out if you're a biology major like me. The library is also gorgeous, and if I'm not studying in the science building, I'm usually there."

- "The gym is looking a little dated, but it will soon be renovated. It's kind of sad, actually, since all the other buildings are really nice and most of them are newer. **Sherwood's sort of the oddball building of the bunch**, but fortunately, not for much longer."

- "**Some buildings are obviously older than others**, but all are really nice. A lot of people complain about Sherwood, but I think it's fine. It has what I need in it, which is all I could ask for."

Q "Most buildings are very spacious and comfortable and look beautiful. **I feel really special being able to study or have classes in really nice facilities**. I think they're also going to re-build the Health Center and Art Center soon, too. They might also put in a new dorm, but that probably won't happen for a while."

Q "As a first-year student, **I was struck by how beautiful everything looked on campus**. All the buildings are well kept and beautiful, and I was pretty surprised to learn about how many more additions and improvements they're making, since it didn't seem like the school really needed it. But all the same, I'm glad. It's always nicer to have newer buildings."

Q "Ironically, the administration seems to be improving all of the non-academic buildings. Though Olin and Maxey [two main buildings for classes] are still in good condition, the school is spending more money now on building another health center and on another athletic center too. I guess it all depends on when and where the money's coming from to make these improvements, but it seems like the money could be better spent on **fixing up the academic buildings**."

Q "**Reid is my favorite place to be**—I really enjoy getting coffee and lunch with friends there. It's much better than the old student building. This one's much more open, has bigger windows, and just has more space all around."

The College Prowler Take On...
Facilities

When it comes to facilities, there are few to no complaints about the quality at Whitman. In fact, the library, science building, and student campus center all were built in the past five years, and plans to rebuild the athletic center and arts center are in progress. Reid Campus Center, which is generally referred to as RCC by most students, or the "SUB" by those who remember the previous student center called the "Student Union Building," is generally the most popular of the newer facilities. Inside, you'll find the student mail center, the book and gift shop, the coffeehouse area (where students and smaller bands or performers put on shows), the Outdoor Programs shop, a T.V. and couch area, café and coffee/ice cream bar, the RCC ballroom, a computer center, one of the art galleries on campus, the Whitman radio station (K-DUB, or KWCW), several offices and study rooms upstairs, the Multicultural Center, student services offices, the Pio (student newspaper) and Bluemoon (student journal) offices, and one of the dark rooms. Probably the shabbiest building is the athletic center—it was designed in the 1970's, most of it is actually underground, and most of it looks like a dungeon.

Many students sometimes feel spoiled with how new and pristine the facilities are, and the high quality definitely makes a difference in how pleasant it is to be in different locations especially the library. There are lots of windows and it doesn't feel like a claustrophobic prison. All-in-all, the up to date facilities contribute to the campus beauty, and make all kinds of tasks—from studying to eating lunch—enjoyable.

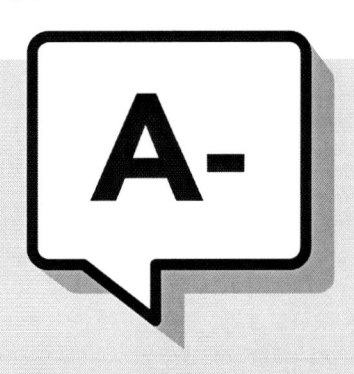

The College Prowler™ Grade on
Facilities: A-

A high Facilities grade indicates that the campus is aesthetically pleasing and well-maintained; facilities are state-of-the-art, and libraries are exceptional. Other determining factors include the quality of both athletic and student centers and an abundance of things to do on campus.

Campus Dining

The Lowdown On...
Campus Dining

Freshman Meal Plan Requirement?
Yes

Meal Plan Average Cost:
$1,940 per semester

Places to Grab a Bite with Your Meal Plan:
Prentiss Dining Hall
Jewett Dining Hall
Lyman Dining Hall
Reid Café (with Flex Dollars – extra purchased "dollars" you can use at RCC or in dining halls that allows you to charge meals to that account without paying each time).

24-Hour On-Campus Eating?
Though there is no particular twenty-four-hour on-campus place to eat, RCC closes at 11:00pm each night, and the Penrose Café located in the basement of the library serves from 8:00pm until 1:00am.

Student Favorites:
Students love the grill and pizza from Reid Café, and most dig the fact that they can get pints of ice cream there, too.

Did You Know?

- Bon Appetit chefs will **specially prepare certain foods for students with dietary restrictions**.
- **Bon Appetit delivers** dinners four nights a week to the Interest House Community in bins, so residents don't necessarily have to go to the dining hall and can order the food they want each week (by submitting a food form).
- If students want to **use their meal plan for raw ingredients**, Bon Appetit lets students fill out "pack out" forms at least a week in advance of the event and Bon Appetit will prepare all the raw items for students to pick up when needed.

Other Options

Reid Center Café is open seven days a week from 8:30 a.m. to 11:00 p.m., featuring Fire & Spice (exhibition cooking), Open Hearth (pizzas and hot sandwiches), and the Whitman Grill. Between the three regular dining halls -- Prentiss, Jewett, and Lyman dining halls -- breakfast is available from 7 a.m. – 10 a.m., lunch from 11:30 a.m.- 1 p.m., and inner from 5:30 p.m. – 7 p.m. Café 41, in Penrose Library, is open from 8 p.m. to 1 a.m.

Students Speak Out On...
Campus Dining

> "The food is better than any of the other colleges I visited as a prospie. It seems like it's always getting better, and the food service people send out surveys all the time to get student feedback."

Q "Though everyone loves to complain about our Bon Appetit food service, **compared to most schools, it's pretty good**. This particularly shows when juniors and seniors return to food service brunch on Saturday and Sunday mornings."

Q "Food is actually pretty good in the dining halls. **One can maintain a very healthy diet really easily**. Bon Appetit even buys local and organic stuff, which is amazing. They do a great job catering to the health nuts and will listen to all requests and fill most of them. Prentiss has a great salad bar, Jewett has the best sandwiches, and Lyman is a nice getaway if you don't want a crowded dining hall for lunch. I also love the omelets."

Q "There is a lot of choices, and **a good vegetarian/vegan selection** [in the dining halls]. The best part about the dining halls is that they take peoples' comments and criticism into consideration when making the food."

Q "**I've never had any complaints**, and it's nice that Whitman doesn't charge students for individual items inside the dining halls like they do at a lot of other schools. It helps that it's all you can eat, but it's frustrating sometimes to feel like you're wasting your money, since meal plans are so expensive and most students don't go to the dining halls often enough to use them all up."

Q "Eating at Reid is popular. One of the meal plan options allows students to charge their campus center meals to their **food service account**, which they use for eating in the dining halls."

Q "**Reid features an espresso bar**, an open hearth pizza oven, a fire and grill area, which weekly alternates between pasta and Asian stir fries, and a grill area for burgers and fries. Also, many students love that they can buy a pint of Haagen Daas here!"

Q "Overall, the food is very good, and **the biggest downfall of food service is that it is very expensive**, and students are required to stay on it for their first couple of years. Students tend to sigh with relief when they move off campus and each semester spend only one-fourth of the price of what they had to spend on campus food."

Q "The food is pretty good. **Anything gets old if you've had it too often.**"

Q "With three dining halls (save for the weekend when only Prentiss is open) **meal times are not too restrictive**."

The College Prowler Take On...
Campus Dining

Like most food made in large quantities, Whitman's food service has its moments of unusual, unidentifiable culinary intrigue, though for the most part, the food is rather delicious. Whitman offers three dining halls: Prentiss, Jewett, and Lyman, which are all open at least five days a week. Prentiss—the largest dining hall—is open most often seven days a week for breakfast, lunch, and dinner; Jewett—the next size down—is open six days a week for breakfast, lunch, and dinner for shorter durations; Lyman is open five days a week for breakfast and lunch only, and is the smallest of the three. Since many students at Whitman are health conscious (there's a large conglomerate of vegetarians and vegans, and the dining halls always offer vegan and vegetarian entrees), the dining halls make it convenient to eat healthily.

In addition to the dining halls, Whitman also offers meals from Reid Campus Center's Whitman Café, which includes a grill, salads, a pizza oven, and a rotating area, which offers anything from Mongolian grill to fajitas. There's also ice cream, baked goods, sodas, organic juice, milk, yogurt, granola, cereal, bagels and toast, salads, soups and several other items. Of course, being a school in the Northwest, Whitman also offers a coffee and ice cream bar with a Barista outside the main café area who makes lattes, espresso, milkshakes or anything your coffee fiend desires. Most students purchase "Flex Dollars" when selecting a meal plan that allows students to charge food items from Reid Café on their Flex accounts, making it easier to eat more variety and outside of the dining halls. For the most part, the food is delicious.

The College Prowler™ Grade on Campus Dining: A-

Our grade on Campus Dining addresses the quality of both school-owned dining halls and independent on-campus restaurants as well as the price, availability, and variety of food.

Off-Campus Dining

The Lowdown On...
Off-Campus Dining

Restaurant Prowler: Popular Places to Eat!

Bangkok 103
Food: Thai
Address: 44 N. College Avenue
College Place, WA 99324
Phone: (509) 522-3007
Cool Features: It's small and secluded—make reservations in advance. Also, they have Thai singers playing on DVD screens in the background.
Price: $10-$15 per person
Hours: Tuesday – Sunday, 3:00 p.m. - dusk

Big Cheese Pizza
499 North Wilbur Avenue
(509) 525-4422
Price: $7-15 per person

La Casita's
Food: Mexican
Address: 315 S. 9th Avenue
Walla Walla, WA 99362
Phone: (509) 522-4941
Fax: None
Cool Features: They offer huge specialty drinks, and you get free dessert if it's your birthday.
Price: $10-15 per person
Hours: Monday-Saturday 1:00 p.m. – 11:00 p.m.

Clarette's
Food: American, anything from omelets to burgers.
Address: 15 S. Touchet Street Walla Walla, WA 99362
Phone: (509) 529-3430
Cool Features: Serves breakfast all day and is owned by a Whitman alumni.
Price: $10 and under per person, unless you get fancy
Hours: Open 7 days a week from 7:00 a.m.-10:00 p.m.

CreekTown Cafe
1129 S. 2nd Ave. Ste. D, Walla Walla, WA 99362 • (509) 522-4777

Merchant's
Food: Italian, coffee, desserts, fresh baked goods (bread, pastries), novelty imported products
Address: 21 E. Main Street Walla Walla, WA 99362
Phone: (509) 525-0900
Fax: None listed
Cool Features: The majority of the products sold here are homemade fresh daily. Waitstaff use playing cards to locate customers and deliver the matching order. Every Wednesday night, Merchant's also stays open for spaghetti night dinner, and there's almost always some form of musical entertainment, either from Whitman or locally.

Merchant's (continued...)
Price: Under $10 per person during the day, for spaghetti dinner $10-15 per person, depending on if you get dessert.
Hours: Monday-Tuesday 6:00 a.m. – 5:00 p.m., Wednesday 6:00 a.m. – 10:00 p.m., Thursday – Saturday 6:00 a.m. – 5:00 p.m., closed Sundays

Shari's
Food: Diner
1401 Lakeside Court Yakima WA 98902 (509) 494-0646
Price: $5-10 per person

Whitehouse Crawford
Food: Expensive (steaks and seafood)
Address: 55 W. Cherry Street Walla Walla, WA 99362
Phone: (509) 525-2222
Cool Features: This restaurant is Walla Walla's leading restaurant in excellence and quality, and usually offers local products (especially onions and wine).
Price: Very expensive anywhere from $25-50 per person
Hours: Saturday – Sunday 5:00 p.m. – 11:00 p.m.

Student Favorites:
- Merchant's
- Bangkok 103
- Any of the local Taco Trucks
- Clarette's
- La Casita's
- Whitehouse Crawford.

24-Hour Eating:
Shari's

Closest Grocery Stores:
Safeway
215 E. Rose Street
Walla Walla, WA 99362
(509) 522-0227

Albertson's
450 N. Wilbur Avenue
Walla Walla, WA 99362
(509) 529-1710

Super One Foods
710 S. 9th Avenue
Walla Walla, WA 99362
(509) 525-8790

Best Pizza:
Big Cheese (especially for cheap deals)

Best Chinese:
Chinese in Walla Walla is actually not very good. You'd be better off going to Bangkok 103 for great Thai food.

Best Breakfast:
Clarette's

Best Wings:
Shari's

Best Healthy:
Merchant's has many healthy options, Creek Town Café.

Best Place to Take Your Parents:
Whitehouse Crawford or Creek Town Café

Fun Facts:
- Walla Walla is **known for its sweet onions**, and new students at Whitman receive a case of them for free the summer before their first year.
- Every Saturday morning from 9:00 a.m. – 12:00 p.m. when the weather is sunny (mainly during spring and early fall), Walla Walla has its **farmer's market** where local farmers and craftsman sell their products and display their work.

Students Speak Out On...
Off-Campus Dining

"For excellent Thai, go to Bangkok 103. For great Mexican, go to any of the taco trucks or La Casita's. Though one doesn't need to venture off campus for food very often since the food on campus really isn't bad at all, it's sometimes really nice to bring a change to one's taste buds."

Q "**Merchants is within walking distance and that's a nice restaurants.** Bangkok (for Thai food) is farther away but worth the drive."

Q "**There are some excellent restaurants for such a small town**. I've really enjoyed checking them all out with friends and family. I'll have to ask my family to come out more often so I can go out to eat more!"

Q "A lot of people rave about it, but **I'd say it's average and overrated**. I've had much better food when I cooked it myself, and I also grew up in a city where there were always lots of really good options for food choices."

Q "Whitehouse Crawford and Creek Town are **good, but expensive.**"

Q "Whitehouse Crawford is a good treat. **It's really expensive though**, so make sure you take your parents so they can treat."

Q "I love Bangkok 103, the Taco Trucks, La Casita, Merchants, and Whitehouse Crawford. There's a lot of diverse food easily available around town. **I think they also put in a Greek restaurant too**."

Q "**There's a lot of good Mexican around here.** For something a little fancier the Whitehouse Crawford is good. And Bangkok 103 in neighboring College Place is GREAT Thai food."

Q "**There's a good sub shop** located down the street from Reid Campus Center within walking distance."

Q "**The best Mexican food I have ever had was at Taco Truck** (El Lagarto). They make everything fresh to order!"

Q "**Clarette's all the way**! It's conveniently located right next to College House and also within walking distance, and it's also owned by a Whitman alum."

The College Prowler Take On...
Off-Campus Dining

Walla Walla, surprisingly, has a lot of delicious food for its size. But generally, students take advantage at some time or another of the good food off campus. There is a lot of diversity in types of foods as well, ranging from Chinese to Thai, Mexican to Italian, or Greek to sheik expensive dinners. The Iceburg is also a Walla Walla favorite and locally famous for its good burgers and thick milk shakes. If you want a really expensive, but really delicious meal—Whitehouse Crawford is the first choice for most, especially since it's a four star restaurant with a very romantic ambiance located right next to the Marcus Whitman Hotel—oh, and it is a great place to take your parents to because of the prices on the menu.

Generally, it's pretty easy to get to any of these restaurants by walking, but it can be a trek. Bangkok 103 is actually located quite a bit off campus, so a car is required for easy transportation, but the rest of the mentioned restaurants are pretty easily accessible by foot. Though it's a bit more expensive to do so, most students take advantage at some point and time of the local restaurants to change up their on campus selections a bit.

A-

The College Prowler™ Grade on
Off-Campus Dining: A-

A high off-campus dining grade implies that off-campus restaurants are affordable, accessible, and worth visiting. Other factors include the variety of cuisine and the availability of alternative options (vegetarian, vegan, Kosher, etc.).

Campus Housing

The Lowdown On...
Campus Housing

Room Types:
Residence Halls include standard or prime rooms for the most part, though private rooms are also available.
- Standard – large, communal bathrooms with toilet stalls and showers (generally where most first-year students end up).
- Prime – bathrooms intended for smaller groups of students are shared (offered for sophomores and older)
- Private – individual rooms and bathrooms are available (this is pretty much exclusive for students living in North Hall, offered for sophomores and older).

Best Dorms:
For quality, Prentiss (all girls); for social life and fun, either Anderson, Jewett.

Worst Dorms:
For a less-happening social life, most say Lyman; for a trek to and from classes, North.

Shared Features:
All of the residence halls at Whitman have rooms with a phone, free voice mail, free internet access, and furniture (including a bed, desk, and dresser).

Shared features (continued...)
The residence halls all have a TV lounge, shared refrigerators, a bike storage room (usually in the basement), and a free laundry room. All residence halls have sprinkler systems for fire safety. Finally, smoking is not allowed in any residence halls or interest houses.

Dormitories:
Anderson Hall
Anderson Hall is a traditional college residence. It houses 140 students, most of whom are first-year students. Anderson features a large central lounge with floor-to-ceiling windows, a fireplace, and a big backyard complete with a sand volleyball court.

Floors: 4 (including basement, where study, storage, and recreational rooms are located).
Total Occupancy: 140
Bathrooms: three per floor, four on the ground level
Co-Ed: Yes
Percentage of Men/Women: It varies each year, but generally it's pretty close to 40% - 60%.
Percentage of First-Year Students: 98% (aside from Residence Life Staff)
Room Types: Standard

Anderson (continued...)
Special Features: Kitchens in each section, laundry room in the basement, recreation center and television with DVD and VCR player in the basement, thin walls, and residential sections are also divided into two sections per floor, each floor being co-ed.

College House
College House, nearest to the Bratton Tennis Center, is a twenty-four-hour quiet hall offering furnished double, triple, or quad apartments. College House is available to sophomores, juniors, and seniors. Students living in College House may choose to do all their own cooking or buy any meal plan. House social activities routinely include movies, dinners with faculty, and outdoor excursions.

Floors: 3 (including basement, storage, common area, recreational room)
Total Occupancy: Approximately 150
Bathrooms: Approximately three per floor
Co-Ed: Yes
Percentage of Men/Women: It varies per year, but generally it's close to 50%/50%
Percentage of First-Year Students: 0%

College (continued...)
Room Types: Standard, apartment style
Special Features: Kitchenettes located in some rooms, no meal plan available, recreational room, laundry room.

Douglas Hall

Douglas Hall is a favorite of sophomores and juniors who like a quiet home for study. Nine suites house only eight students each, an arrangement which fosters a more private lifestyle, as well as close ties among residents. There are two bathrooms, a kitchenette, lounge, and laundry facilities in each suite, and ten single rooms available in the hall. The suites are built around a central courtyard that is the site of barbecues and informal gatherings.
Floors: 3 (including basement, storage, common area, recreational room)
Total Occupancy: Approximately 150
Bathrooms: Approximately three per floor
Co-Ed: Yes
Percentage of Men/Women: It varies per year, but generally it's close to 50%/50%
Percentage of First-Year Students: 0%

Douglas (continued...)
Room Types: Standard
Special Features: Rooms are located in clusters with kitchenettes in each cluster

Jewett Hall

This traditional residence houses close to 180 first year students. It is nestled on the northeast fringe of Ankeny Field, 100 yards from Penrose Library. A prime location for activities such as ultimate frisbee and outdoor studying, Jewett also has spacious lounges with kitchen space, a recreation room, and a free laundry room.

Floors: 4 (including basement, storage, common area, recreational room)
Total Occupancy: 180
Bathrooms: Approximately three per floor
Co-Ed: Yes
Percentage of Men/Women: It varies each year, but generally it's pretty close to 40% - 60%.
Percentage of First-Year Students: 98% (aside from Residence Life Staff)
Room Types: Standard
Special Features: Kitchens on each floor, laundry rooms, recreation center and television with DVD and VCR, and residential sections are also divided by sex.

Lyman House

Lyman House, a mixed-class hall, is known for its old-fashioned charm and family-like atmosphere. The fireplace in its main lounge serves as a focal point for informational gatherings. Lyman houses ninety-nine students in two-room suites, so roommates can arrange shared sleeping and living rooms, or each have separate spaces. Lyman, which is the oldest residence hall on campus, underwent a renovation in 1997. It has its own small dining hall that attracts most of its residents for weekday lunches and dinners.

Floors: 3 (including basement, storage, common area, recreational room)
Total Occupancy: 180
Bathrooms: Approximately three per floor
Co-Ed: Yes
Percentage of Men/Women: It varies each year, but generally it's pretty close to 40% - 60%.
Percentage of First-Year Students: this also varies per year, but generally it's about 30% (aside from Residence Life Staff)
Room Types: Standard
Special Features: Dining hall on bottom floor, two-room dorms, recreational room and laundry room.

Marcus House

Marcus House, located directly across from the Reid Campus Center, is another choice for upper-class students. A shady yard with a stream and pond provide an idyllic setting for quiet conversation and studying. Indoors, there is a large kitchen and eating area and in the backyard has a basketball court. The house offers singles, doubles, and triples for up to 27 students.

Floors: 3 (including basement, storage, common area, recreational room)
Total Occupancy: Approximately 150
Bathrooms: Approximately 3 per floor
Co-Ed: Yes
Percentage of Men/Women: It varies per year, but generally it's close to 50%/50%
Percentage of First-Year Students: 0%
Room Types: Standard
Special Features: Large kitchen available for residents, laundry room, and recreation room

North Hall

North Hall is a choice for about seventy returning and transfer students who want their own room, but still enjoy being part of a larger living community. Nestled in a residential neighborhood on the northern edge of campus, North Hall features a huge yard with a pond. North Hall has the widest hallways and the largest single rooms on campus. Residents also enjoy playing pool in the game room, watching movies with friends, cooking Saturday night dinners together, and talking in one of the lounges.

Floors: 3 (including basement, storage, common area, recreational room)
Total Occupancy: Approximately 150
Bathrooms: Approximately three per floor
Co-Ed: Yes
Percentage of Men/Women: It varies per year, but generally it's close to 50%/50%
Percentage of First-Year Students: 0%
Room Types: Standard
Special Features: Large kitchen available for residents, laundry room, and recreation room

Prentiss Hall

Prentiss Hall with its brick facade and tall windows is a stately residence built in 1926 and completely renovated in 1992. Prentiss features an attractive arrangement of inner and outer rooms for all doubles, many study rooms, and an AV seminar room. About 150 women live here including sorority members and new students.

Floors: 3 (including basement, storage, common area, recreational room)
Total Occupancy: 150
Bathrooms: Approximately 3 per floor
Co-Ed: No
Percentage of Men/Women: 0% men, 100% women
Percentage of First-Year Students: this also varies per year, but generally it's about 40% (aside from Residence Life Staff)
Room Types: Standard
Special Features: Piano downstairs, recreational room, houses sororities, quiet and pristine rooms and floors.

Tamarac House

Tamarac House, a three-story apartment building turned residence hall, and is the latest campus gateway to the world of nature. Perched on the corner of Park and Main, Tamarac is home to twenty students with a deep and abiding love for outdoor adventure.

Floors: 5 (including basement, storage, common area, recreational room)
Total Occupancy: 20
Bathrooms: Approximately two per floor
- Co-Ed: Yes
- Percentage of Men/Women: It varies per year, but generally it's close to 50%/50%
- Percentage of First-Year Students: 0%, or close to 0%
- Room Types: Standard
- Special Features: Focus of house is directed towards outdoor activities

Undergrads on Campus:
59%

Number of Dormitories:
8

Available for Rent:
Mini fridges!

Cleaning Service?
All dorms have a cleaning service, generally it comes once a week, but in some areas, it comes once every two weeks. The custodial staff is very warm, and does a fantastic job keeping all the areas so clean.

You Get
A bed (that can be lofted or bunked upon request unless in Jewett), desk, chair, dresser, closet or wardrobe, mirrors, free campus and local phone, Ethernet, wireless, or broadband Internet connections.

Also Available
Private, single room upon request (though very unlikely to receive as a first-year unless with special circumstances), more items of furniture if requested from the Physical Plant and if extra items are available.

Students Speak Out On...
Campus Housing

> "Whitman seems to place students really well, even though students do send in their first choices of dorms. If you don't get your first choice, don't worry too much because you may end up living in a really great situation that you didn't think would fit you as well."

Q "As for choosing a place to live, it really all depends on what you're looking for. **If you want quiet, either Lyman, Marcus or North, if you want a rowdy first-year experience, either Anderson or Jewett**. And if you're a really tidy girl who doesn't care about seeing men that often, then Prentiss is the way to go."

Q "**Each residence hall has its own personality**, but that changes from year-to-year with the residents. The important thing to remember is that you will have an amazing freshman year even if you don't get your first choice for housing. Be open-minded!"

Q "**Jewett is the best first year dorm**. If you want to get a 'college experience' It's a good place to start. Prentiss (all girls) and North (off in 'Booniesville') are not most peoples' number one pick."

Q "As far as options for residence, the two first-year co-ed residence halls, Anderson and Jewett are probably the least nicest ones on campus. **Prentiss (all girls [and where sorority members live])**, and Lyman are a step up."

Q "All dorms are nice, despite the fact that each has its reputation. The reputations **(Lyman is the dorm for anti-socials,** North is a long way away, etc.) are fairly unfounded."

Q "**Definitely avoid North**! It's SO far away from campus, and it's a pain to walk back and forth, especially in winter. I used to bum rides from friends to campus, even though the walk really isn't that long because it was so cold to walk. And a lot of people end up 'disappearing' once they move to North. It's harder to stay as 'in' to the social scene there, and most people who live there are introverted and want a quiet, not-so-happening place."

Q "**Most students, no matter where they live, end up finding the niche they probably would have found otherwise**. People with common interests attract each other, so I think, though it may take more time for some than others, most people do end up finding their places eventually no matter where they live."

Q "Even though [North] is looked upon as **haunted or taboo**, it was really nice to have my own room. I got more studying done that way."

Q "**Lyman is a hall that carries some stigma**, but for people who are looking for a more laid back living environment it's perfect. Prentiss, the all women's dorm, is very nice, but it is also crazy."

Q "The Interest House Community is a great place to live for **a cozy home atmosphere,** and a chance to mingle with people of shared interests."

Q "I've loved living in the IHC. This will be my second semester, and it's infinitely better living in a household situation than in the dorms. I don't think I could handle living in the dorms again—I just **never felt like I had any privacy**, especially in Anderson where the walls are thin and the girls are really gossipy."

Q "The dorms are really nice. I'd say **aesthetically Anderson and Prentiss are the nicest**. There's not really one to avoid, it depends on your living preferences."

The College Prowler Take On...
Campus Housing

Whitman's residence halls are very high quality, and they each have their quirks. Opinions of the best dorms vary. North, Douglass, Marcus, and College House are all options for upper classmen (Lyman is one as well; it's mixed between first-years and upper classmen), and these halls are also high in quality. North, the off-campus hall, used to be a hospital, and has somewhat of a stigma attached to it, though the rooms are more spacious and many have their own bathrooms. The Interest House Community, a collection of eleven Whitman-owned houses, is a unique opportunity for students to live in a household setting that matches or relates to their personal interests. Houses include the Fine Arts House, La Casa Hispana (the Spanish House), the Outhouse (Environmental House), the Co-Op (Community Service House), the Global House (Political House), Das Deutsche Haus (the German House), La Maison Francaise (the French House), the Asian Studies House, the Writing House, the TEK House (Japanese House), and the MECCA House (Multi-Ethnic Center for Cultural Awareness). Each house is staffed with a Resident Assistant (R.A.), and puts on campus-wide and IHC-wide activities to foster campus life. Generally, the Interest Houses are only offered after your first year, though exceptions have been made.

Be prepared to deal with and perhaps defend the different reputations of each dorm and the different challenges of each: for first years, Jewett has pull-out couch beds, Anderson's walls are paper-thin, Lyman is notoriously quiet and doesn't throw many, if any, parties, and estrogen-ridden Prentiss leaps at any hint of testosterone; for sophomores and up, the IHC tends to stay centralized and united (but not necessarily exclusive to non-IHC members), Douglass is pretty quiet, College House is somewhat detached from campus because residents are not on food service generally, and it's off campus. North is a great escape from campus life, and Marcus is fairly nerdy and not as sociable as other dorms.

B+

The College Prowler™ Grade on Campus Housing: B+

A high Campus Housing grade indicates that dorms are clean, well-maintained, and spacious. Other determining factors include variety of dorms, proximity to classes, and social atmosphere.

Off-Campus Housing

The Lowdown On...
Off-Campus Housing

Undergrads in Off-Campus Housing:
41%

Best Time to Look for a Place:
As fall semester is ending—many students go abroad for spring and need someone to take over their places.

Average Rent:
Studio: $350 per month
1BR: $450 per month
2BR: $755 per month

Popular Areas:
Clinton Court houses a lot of students (though residences are not exclusively from Whitman College), and near the fraternities.

For Assistance Contact:
Mason Smith, Director of Communications
Web: www.whitman.edu/news/bios/#msmith
E-mail: smithmm@whitman.edu

Students Speak Out On...
Off-Campus Housing

> "I personally never bothered with it. On-campus housing is pretty diverse and satisfactory, but I can see moving for financial reasons. There are a lot of apartments in the near vicinity [like Clinton Court]."

Q "**On-campus housing is required through sophomore year**. Most people move off-campus for junior and senior year though, so it is available and must be worth it."

Q "I know I'll appreciate the option when the time comes, but for now, I don't really care either way. I like being able to live with my friends in the dorms, both guys and girls, and it's a nice communal area where you're guaranteed to find people. I'm sure it'll feel different when I live in a house, but it'll be a nice change of pace to live with my better friends in our own place and feel like we're more independent. **Oh yeah, and no RAs**—that'll be nice when we feel like kicking back a few."

Q "It's pretty convenient. **As long as you're pretty close to campus, it's a good idea**. I couldn't wait to move off campus—it was so much easier to get a place with my friends and just live our lives. It's nice knowing Res Life won't sweep through and fine us if something's not clean. I feel much more independent living on my own, which is pretty hard to do considering Whitman's size and location."

Q "**It's easy to live off campus**. It's probably worth it too, and cheaper, especially since you get to live with your friends and be off food service."

Q "It's easy to find and affordable. Plus, **you don't have to be on a meal plan**, which is very nice. I felt much more independent and less tied-down by Whitman's regulations in my own place, plus I got to live with all of my close friends. It's actually cheaper, if you do it right, to live in a house off campus than to live on campus."

Q "I'll be a junior next year, and I can't wait to have a house off campus. My friends and I found our house last spring, and we've already started moving our stuff into it. The thing that I like most about having my own house is that it's a reliably quiet environment where I can study and work on school-related things without disruption. It's hard to work on homework in the dorms, especially as a freshman, because **people are always socializing and leaving their doors open**, so you can come talk to anyone. It's much more distracting, and since I know that my friends live with me, I don't have to take every opportunity to talk to them."

Q "**Be careful about where you rent from**. Housing is pretty good, but it can be expensive, depending on the quality of the house and where it's located."

Q "I've always found it to be easier to just stay on campus. I don't have to worry about finding a house that's close enough to all my classes or in good enough shape so that it doesn't require a lot of repairs that I don't have the time to do. **It's nice not having to worry about rent and bills**, but I guess in a way, this set up sort of prevents students from 'growing up' more, since living on campus means most things are taken care of for you and you don't have to worry about the things most people worry about, like cleaning."

The College Prowler Take On...
Off-Campus Housing

Most students choose to live off campus after their sophomore year (since sophomores are still required to live on campus unless they petition otherwise), and it's generally pretty convenient. Whitman owns quite a few off-campus houses, and students who want a Whitman-owned house enter into a lottery for specific ones. It's also pretty easy to find houses that aren't Whitman-owned around campus that are inexpensive to rent, and many of these houses have been passed down from Whitman group to Whitman group of students over the years. Many of the landlords also understand that many Whitman students need places to live and desire off-campus housing as well, so most landlords are understanding when it comes to student's needs.

In terms of off-campus housing being worthwhile, rent in Walla Walla is actually very reasonable, and in most cases, cheaper than the housing costs on Whitman campus (though the housing costs on campus also include free cleaning services, furniture, and the Physical Plant to take care of repairs or needed furniture for students). Some students consider the Interest Houses off campus, and in that sense, it's also worth it to live a bit more off campus. Other students don't bother with off-campus housing. Overall, off-campus housing is a definite option, but just make sure to be open-minded about where you end up if you enter into a lottery, and not too choosy about new, high quality houses.

B+

The College Prowler™ Grade on Off-Campus Housing: B+

A high grade in Off-Campus Housing indicates that apartments are of high quality, close to campus, affordable, and easy to secure.

Diversity

The Lowdown On...
Diversity

White:
77.6%

Asian or Pacific Islander:
7.3%

Hispanic:
3.2%

African American:
1.3%

American Indian:
0.8%

Unknown:
7.4%

Minority Clubs:
Black Student Union (BSU)

Vietnamese Culture Club (VCC)

Asian Culture Association (ACA)

Club Latino

American Indian Association.

Political Activity

Whitman is a very active school politically. Most students are liberal, both socially and politically. Students are caring and active in protests and forums, though these don't happen in an incredible abundance. If asked, most students would have and be able to explain their opinions, political, and social views on almost any issue. Students like to keep themselves informed, and they often like to get up and arms about even the smaller issues, like debates over the student e-mail list serve.

Gay Tolerance

Tolerance for homosexuality at Whitman is very strong, especially considering the strong religious affiliations of Walla Walla (it's a Seventh Day Adventist community). Most students are very tolerant, accepting, and open with their feelings towards homosexuality, though I imagine some students still have some difficulty with these issues. Generally speaking though, Whitman students are highly tolerant of homosexuality, or any type of sexuality for that matter.

Most Popular Religions

There seems to be a divide between agnostic or atheist students and religious students, mainly Christian, Jewish, or Catholic. Religion does not seem to be too much of the focus on campus, though it is generally accepted; Bible groups have been created before, and there's a very active Jewish group on campus called "Shalom".

Economic Status

There's a large variety of economic status at Whitman, though lower-class population percentages are smaller. Though Whitman tries to cater to all students, the school does, unfortunately, have a reputation as a school for the "rich, white kids". Fortunately, more student organizations have recently been created to help students with less prosperous financial backgrounds adjust to Whitman and provide on-going support.

Students Speak Out On...
Diversity

> "Diversity? There is not so much, although the school does a good job of trying to make it so with resources. The Intercultural Center, Black Student Union (BSU), Club Latino, MECCA Multi-Ethnic House, and all of the international students add a lot of flavor."

Q "Whitman is as diverse as **vanilla ice cream**."

Q "It's appalling in many ways how un-diverse Whitman is—it's pretty sad. I came from a really diverse city, and **most of the kids who go here don't seem to have a clue what it's like to be in the 'real world' that isn't so white**. It's frustrating, but I deal with it in the ways that I can, and I have supportive friends."

Q "**There is certainly diversity in lifestyles and beliefs** (religion, sexuality, life choices), but not so much in the classic sense of racial diversity."

Q "Many students at Whitman are tired of hearing how Whitman is not diverse, but the problem with Whitman is that if they could make those few minority students feel that they belong to the Whitman community, to me, diversity would not be a problem. But the thing is that **even those few diverse or working-class students either end up leaving or just sucking it up**, so that tells you there's a problem."

Q "**Sadly Whitman is not at all diverse**, not only in ethnicity, but in class too."

Q "**There's really NO diversity here**! I rarely see a diverse group of faces in most of my classes, and though it doesn't seem to affect the kind of class discussions that take place, I know the views of this school are lacking because they aren't at all encompassing as a more diverse school would be."

Q "**There's a wide variety of interests and talents**, so that brings some diversity. It's nice to be in such an accepting environment when it comes to peoples' personal interests and what they've done before they came to Whitman. But I can honestly say that's pretty much the only form of diversity."

Q "**There's much diversity activity-wise**, and students seem to try to make up for the lack of racial diversity by putting on a wide variety of events and programs."

Q "**I have several friends who aren't from the dominant class**, and they're all fed up with how non-diverse Whitman is. Most of them have strongly considered leaving at one time or another, and I'm glad most of them haven't because the few of them bring a lot to the school and are very active. If it weren't for these few students, Whitman would be even more homogenous and much more boring."

Q "Whitman is **a pretty hard place to adjust to** unless you're used to a predominantly white, middle-upper class environment."

The College Prowler Take On...
Diversity

Oh, diversity! Whitman's nickname is actually "White-Man," which may provide some insight into the diversity there. Most students really recognize that this is a problem, but many don't do much about it for whatever reason. It seems as though students and the administration know the lack of diversity is a problem, but people are unsure of how to go about improving, fixing, or dealing with the issue. Though these resources are available, generally students who already are aware of the issues take advantage of them (primarily minority students or international students)—people who are aware of the issues enough to take action about them (not necessarily students who really need to be educated on why diversity is important at Whitman). Many forums and events are held that foster diversity and cultural awareness (such as race/racism forums or the Imagine Festival), but often (particularly minority students) feel these events are "preaching to the converted" because students who are aware enough about the lack of diversity, and most willing to act on it, are those who attend rather than students who ignore the issues attached to the lack of diversity. Beyond race and class, students themselves have pretty eclectic personalities. Students also bring these interests and form new activities on campus. Racial diversity is largely lacking, however. In fact, many students with different racial backgrounds have often felt it difficult to adjust to the homogeny of Whitman. Most students agree that personality-wise and interest-wise, Whitman is a diverse place. In terms of other forms of diversity? You'll be hard-pressed to find much of it.

The College Prowler™ Grade on
Diversity: D

A high grade in Diversity indicates that ethnic minorities and international students have a notable presence on campus and that students of different economic backgrounds, religious beliefs, and sexual preferences are well-represented.

Guys & Girls

The Lowdown On...
Guys & Girls

Men Undergrads:
47.5%

Women Undergrads:
52.5%

Birth Control Available?
Yes, the Health Center sells condoms for ten cents (and the dorms often have them for free), the "Morning After" pill, and birth control available through the physician on campus. Planned Parenthood is also located not too far from campus, and they offer free birth control if the requester qualifies.

Most Prevalent STDs on Campus
Human Papilloma Virus (HPV), Genital Herpes, Chlamydia, and Molluscum Contagiosum.

Social Scene

Most Whitman students are very sociable and excited to be in a new social environment, especially first-year students. By the end of freshman year, most new students know everyone in their class and in the entire school. It is a rarity for students to walk by each other and recognize each other's faces, though they may not have been formally introduced. Students rapidly get to know each other by name or reputation, and students do a lot of bonding and mingling with other students from class in order to meet people outside their living situation (students who are older seem to use this tactic to meet others more than first-years). After freshman year, the social circle seems to expand and students get to know more than just their former-freshman peers, either through classes, sports or where they end up living. It's a very social campus, and students spend a lot of their free time talking with one another and having coffee or playing sports.

Hookups or Relationships?

There are many hook-ups, although relationships also have a pretty strong presence on campus, as well. Most often, hook-ups seem to be more popular with freshman and somewhat with sophomores. Generally, relationships don't start until after freshman year, though couples who start together during freshman year often end up staying together all four years. In all reality, there probably aren't as many relationships as there seem to be; relationships are very widely known and students who keep themselves updated in the "couples/dating" circuit know who's with whom for the most part, and who is available. It's hard to keep relationships on the down-low, though hook-ups can generally stay pretty anonymous unless they take place in more public areas with a gossipy crowd.

Best Place to Meet Guys/Girls

Many times, guys and girls meet each other at the fraternity parties, especially at the beginning of the year. Whitman sponsors a lot of parties in the fall (Country-Ho Downs on Ankeny Field or 80's Dances in the dorms), so students, especially first-years, have many chances to mingle. Aside from this, many students also meet their significant others in classes, and use this context as a base to share their personal interests and find something in common to strike up conversations about.

After freshman year, students have the best luck meeting other students at frat parties and music events, although many students also meet people through their friends or other connections (from classes, clubs or organizations, friends of friends, etc.).

As far as meeting people who aren't from Whitman, this is quite a bit more challenging because most students don't spend enough time off campus. Though some students have met people at the local clubs and bars (like Barnaby's or Rosita's), it's much more challenging, and much less likely that a student will date or be involved with someone who doesn't attend Whitman. This is probably the case because life at Whitman is very "Whitman centralized" presenting more of a challenge for those who aren't engulfed in the Whitman environment. Some students have met non-Whitman people from Walla Walla College or Walla Walla Community College, though students from these other schools rarely come to the Whitman campus unless it's for open musical events or if dances are taking place.

Dress Code

Dress code definitely depends on the occasion. Most Whitman students don't seem to care too much about their appearance and seem to like this aspect of their whole image as more of a hippie-type dresser, but dress code definitely varies depending on the social group and event. Many girls don't wear make-up or follow clothing trends, though this does happen from time-to-time. Most sorority girls do care quite a bit about how they look and get dolled up to go to anything from classes to parties, and guys mainly don't care too much either way. There are guys who do dress stylishly and who obviously care about how they look, but this is generally the case when parties are happening or for events where more people will be there and not necessarily always consistent. People seem to prefer comfort over appearance, especially for classes. It's not uncommon for students to roll out of bed in their PJs and just go, especially during finals—then hygiene also takes a back seat. But for parties or big events, most students will be well put-together, and sometimes, not as recognizable as they are in class.

Top Three Places to Find Hotties:
- TKE House, but pretty much any of the fraternity houses.
- Sporting events, especially basketball in fall and ultimate Frisbee in spring.
- Any large party, be it on campus in the dorms or off campus at someone's house.

Top Places to Hookup:
- Any frat party.
- Dorm parties, especially for first-years, are hook-up frenzies.
- Off-campus parties—Whitman students who live in and throw parties at their off-campus homes usually nickname their houses, and the names of hot spots usually spread pretty quickly (especially "The Monstrosity" "The Fishbowl," and "The Bakery").
- At and after school sponsored dances (only a handful of these each year).
- Very top floor of the library, so it's happened only a handful of times.

Students Speak Out On...
Guys & Girls

> "Most guys at Whitman were pretty attractive, especially if you like the more rugged looking guys. A lot of them are like scruffier Greek Gods, and it's great in spring when they all walk around without their shirts."

- "I hate generalizations, but basically **everyone here is very nice and intelligent**, and typically quite attractive."

- "For whatever reason, it seems like **guys have a harder time approaching girls who they like**. It's never uncommon for students to have several crushes on fellow students at a time, but because life moves so fast here, and because it's so much extra effort to have a relationship, most students don't seem to act on these crushes unless they're really ready to take on the extra challenge they present. I've never been in a relationship at Whitman, and they seem to be all over the place, so I guess there are some people willing to take on the extra time."

- "**There are a handful of guys who I find attractive**, and that seems to be enough for me. My interaction with them varies depending on if I have classes with them or if we talked at parties, but otherwise, it seems like it's harder for girls to meet guys than for guys to meet girls. The ratio is skewed in their [guys'] favor!"

- "My mom commented that it's the place where **healthy-looking handsome folks** go."

Q "It seems that Whitman girls go after guys **a lot and the girls are cool**."

Q "There are a number of really hot girls, and **a lot of them are sporty and dig the outdoors**, which is sweet. Most of the hotties are from sororities, but there are some hot Indy girls too. I just don't have much interaction with the Indy girls because I'm in a frat, so most of the girls I meet are through inter-Greek functions with sororities, which is fine with me since that's where most of the finer ladies are."

Q "**Whitman is the school of nerds** who, finding themselves surrounded by other nerds upon arrival, suddenly feel cool."

Q "Typically, **students haven't seemed to care about their appearances**, but more recently I've seen much more makeup and fashionable clothes on younger students than I remembered."

Q "The girls are quite attractive, and most have a personality, opinions, and **deeper conversational skills than your typical valley girl**. There are some brain-dead, dud girls, but most of them are really smart and down to Earth. You have to be if you're a Whitman student, otherwise it's hard to keep up with everything."

Q "**Guys are nice**, not very attractive, and do not approach girls at all."

Q "**I wish it was easier to have a relationship with a guy**. I've been involved with lots of great, cute guys, but a lot of them aren't looking for a relationship, which sucks. In a way it's good though, because I don't know if I have the time for it anyway, and I'm going abroad in the fall, so I won't be here either."

Q "Most guys at Whitman were pretty attractive, especially if you like **the more rugged looking guys**. A lot of them are like scruffier Greek Gods, and it's great in spring when they all walk around without their shirts."

The College Prowler Take On...
Guys and Girls

Many of the sorority girls on campus are well-primped and wear many of the latest fashions, but, believe it or not, these girls do have personalities); most hippie girls have treads or walk in sandals or wear hemp and peasant tops with long skirts; most of the quieter girls dress more conservatively in simpler styles. There are, of course, the stand-out, attractive girls, and they are notorius on campus. In general, however, the girls do tend to be pretty good-looking, and those who take better care in their appearance vary. For the most part, it's the girls who complain that there aren't "any decent guys," and since girls outnumber guys at Whitman, this is sometimes a primary source of frustration for females. As is the case with girls, many of the guys are nerds, or at least "closet nerds." Most of the more attractive guys don't stay single long or are highly sought after by several women—many of the "good ones" are quickly swooped up by boy-crazy women. Many of the more attractive guys end up in fraternities, and since Greek life tends to socialize internally, it's pretty difficult for non-Greek women to have a relationship with a Greek-affiliated guy. There are several attractive guys who are known across campus to be universally attractive, but generally, girls feel the guys are not as attractive on a whole as they are elsewhere. If you're a straight female, be prepared for some competition for the more attractive guys on campus. However, what the men lack in attractiveness, they make up for in personality, sense of humor, and brains.

B-

The College Prowler™ Grade on Guys: B-

A high grade for Guys indicates that the male population on campus is attractive, smart, friendly, and engaging, and that the school has a decent ratio of guys to girls.

B

The College Prowler™ Grade on Girls: B

A high grade for Girls not only implies that the women on campus are attractive, smart, friendly, and engaging, but also that there is a fair ratio of girls to guys.

Athletics

The Lowdown On...
Athletics

Athletic Division:
NCAA Division III

Number Of Male Undergraduate Varsity Athletes:
113

Percent Of Total Male Undergraduate Students:
18%

Number Of Female Undergraduate Varsity Athletes:
116

Percent Of Total Female Undergraduate Students:
14%

Intercollegiate Varsity Sports

Men's Teams:
Cross Country
Soccer
Golf
Basketball
Alpine Skiing
Nordic Skiing
Swimming
Baseball
Tennis
Golf

Women's Teams:
Cross Country
Soccer
Golf
Volleyball
Winter –
Basketball
Alpine Skiing
Nordic Skiing
Swimming
Tennis
Golf

Club Sports:
Rugby (men)
Snowboarding (men/women)
Fencing (men/women)
Lacrosse (men/women)
Cycling (men/women)
Ultimate Frisbee (men/women)

Intramurals:
Football (men/women)
Volleyball (men/women)
Softball (men/women)
Basketball (men/women)
Ultimate Frisbee (men/women)
Rugby (men/women)
Lacrosse (men/women)

Fields:
Ankeny (in the middle of everything and hard to miss), Whitman Athletic Complex (farther off campus), Science Field (behind the Science building).

Getting Tickets:
Tickets are needed for sporting events, and in the rare occasion that they are, they are well advertised and sold generally inside RCC.

School Mascot:
Fighting Missionaries

Most Popular Sports:
Intramural sports of all varieties are the most popular on campus. IM football is hugely popular, and gets students integrated into the sports culture right off the bat in the fall. Ultimate Frisbee is also another popular sport, since many students play Frisbee recreationally, anyway. The basketball games have been known to get pretty populated, but the games aren't incredibly exciting unless you know students on the team to cheer them on. Lacrosse can also get pretty popular during the spring, and Whitman's cycling team usually places strongly in national competitions, too. Students almost always seem to know when sporting events are taking place, and some make efforts to go and see them, but generally, they aren't the first priority.

Overlooked Teams:
Women's rugby recently came into existence over these past few years, and seems to be getting more and more popular. Swimming is usually poorly attended because there aren't many bleachers by the pool for spectators. And baseball games usually aren't very well attended because the field is a bit of a trek off-campus. Also, rock-climbing is widely popular, and probably popular enough to become its own club or IM sport, but it hasn't budged from its status as an extra-curricular.

Gyms/Facilities:
Sherwood Athletic Center
The most frequently used athletic facility. The cardio room has treadmills, bikes, rowing, machines. The weight room is actually very spacious, and well equipped with both machines and free weights. There are two basketball courts, one with a newly installed wood floor, the other painted concrete. There are six or so racquetball and squash ball courts, generally full of students in the afternoons. Inside the locker rooms, there are communal showers, several rows of lockers, toilets and sinks, and a sauna, which gives the place some bonus points quality-wise. There is one aerobics studio where aerobics classes are held, as well. If you like working out in the afternoons though, be prepared for long lines for cardio machines and a crowded weight room. Despite its scruffiness, and the ugliness of its exterior, Sherwood provides the bare-minimum of what most students need in terms of an athletic center. Fortunately, plans to renovate and remodel Sherwood are already in progress, and a new athletic center is scheduled to be completed soon.

Bratton Indoor Tennis Center
This center was built exclusively for tennis courts and houses four indoor courts with a balcony for spectators.

Ankeny Tennis Courts
Three outdoor courts reside next to Ankeny field where both tennis classes and matches take place most often.

Ankeny Field
This huge field provides areas for sports ranging from soccer to lacrosse, although it can get quite muddy, and torn up from all the teams who play out there.

Whitman Athletic Center
There are three more fields out here where many ultimate Frisbee teams compete and practice, along with two baseball diamonds and an outdoor track.

Best Place to Take a Walk:
Pioneer Park is not too far away from campus, and it's a beautiful, easy walk where students can also look at the aviary. Walking around campus is also very pleasant, and the neighboring residential areas are quiet, quaint, and charming.

Students Speak Out On...
Athletics

"Definitely play an IM or club sport! It was really nice after a long day of classes to let loose some stress and have fun with friends. Plus, people are accepting in most IM sports and recognize that students have all kinds of athletic abilities, despite the fact that many IM sports are pretty intense and serious."

- "IM sports, especially football, are **pretty huge.**"

- "IM sports are very popular at Whitman, particularly football, which is a huge draw in the hall that gets all dorms involved, as well as **frats, sororities, and independent teams.**"

- "Generally speaking, **Whitman's varsity teams are not very good.** Our ski and snowboard teams have won national awards and though not usually successful in their league, the basketball team really rallies to get people to come to its games."

- "Sure, it's always fun to go to some of the sporting events like the basketball games, and sometimes I miss having a big football team and a distinct football season (my high school was really into it). But you take what you can get and trade for other things. **It's nice that there are so many IM teams and club sports** so anyone can play if they want to, even if it does mean we don't have a huge, packed stadium."

- "Men's varsity basketball is probably **the most popular of the varsity sports** and IM football of the IM sports."

- "**Varsity sports are pretty much a joke**. It's sad, but we're certainly not known for our varsity sports teams. We're pretty competitive in some sports, like with cycling and ultimate Frisbee, but not so much with the more mainstream sports such as baseball or basketball."

- "Varsity sports aren't very big, although **the basketball games get pretty good turnouts**. IM sports seem bigger to me, and they're really fun."

- "I'd say that IM sports are probably better attended by spectators than varsity sports. To my knowledge, **people get more involved (as spectators) in the IM teams** than varsity."

- "Varsity sports don't attract too much attention **outside of their own participants**."

- "Though we don't have huge varsity sports, I really appreciate how **most students at Whitman are athletically active**. It's really nice to be in a place where people are about exercising their minds and bodies. Plus, it's really fun to play IM sports, and it's a great way to meet people you haven't met before."

- "It is nice to participate in sports, as **there is an overall vigorousness for physical activity** and healthy lifestyle at Whitman, but there is no hierarchical structure in the social scene and on campus involving sports parts."

- "It seems like **Whitman is not very competitive and into sports**. Whitman is more into academics, which is not a bad thing, but at the same time when your sports team sucks it doesn't raise up Whitman pride or spirit."

- "I feel like Whitman the school takes varsity sports very seriously; **they like to brag about them when possible**, but I feel that since the focus of the school is so much more on the academic side (no sports scholarships, for example), people tend to get much more excited about IM—since so many people participate and basically anyone can join a team."

The College Prowler Take On...
Athletics

Though students at Whitman take part in all forms of athletics and exercise, varsity sports are not a high priority in students' lives. In fact, most intramural sports are more popular than varsity sports, and students get pretty into IM athletics. Teams often dress up in costumes and create team cheers rather than support the handful of varsity sports on campus. When a sports program is not very competitive, there is just not a lot to get excited about, therefore that void has to be filled, and IM sports are a pretty good filler. Whitman has nine IM sports, overshadowing the eleven varsity sports. In addition, Whitman also has club sports ranging from co-ed fencing to co-ed ultimate Frisbee.

Most students participate in some form of athletics, primarily because most students at Whitman care about exercise or outdoor athletics like hiking, skiing, or bicycling. Athletics generally are a secondary aspect to Whitman life, the first being academics. The most popular varsity sport on campus is basketball and it's football for intramurals. Overall, sports are a great way for people to meet each other and get to know more students outside of their living situations, but by no means are an essential aspect of Whitman life, especially to socialize.

The College Prowler™ Grade on Athletics: B

A high grade in Athletics indicates that students have school spirit, that sports programs are respected, that games are well-attended, and that intramurals are a prominent part of student life.

Nightlife

The Lowdown On...
Nightlife

Club Crawler:
It's at least some consolation that Walla Walla has some places to dance, but it's unfortunate that most of them are pretty shady places. Sometimes students have parties over there, but for the most part, students stay centralized on campus. Here are the names of the two best places to go to dance.

Barnaby's
1817 Issacs Avenue
Walla Walla, WA 99362
This is a great place for the twenty-one and older crowds to go for drinks and dancing. It's the only place that offers a really great dance floor and good drinks, and seniors often have their parties here.
Friday & Saturday Happy Hour
(Ladies drink free)

Rosita's
201 E. Main Street
Walla Walla, WA 99362
(509) 525-6361
This is a good place to go for good hip-hop music and the DJs usually aren't too bad. They sponsor eighteen and older parties as well as exclusive twenty-one and older events. It varies depending on the night, but many students have enjoyed going here. Friday & Saturday Happy Hour (discounted drinks)

Bar Prowler:
There aren't too many places for students to go for drinks, but of the more well known are the following two places.

Brew Pub
26 Boyer Avenue
Walla Walla, WA 99362

Green Lantern
1606 E. Isaacs Avenue
Walla Walla, WA 99362
(509) 525-6303

Other Places to Check Out:
McFeely's Tavern
Coffee Bean
Coffee Perk
Starlight Bowling Alley

Favorite Drinking Games:
Beer Pong
Card Games (Kings, A$$hole)
Quarters

Student Favorites:
Barnaby's
Rosita's
Green Lantern
Campus parties (especially at the TKE house)

Useful Resources for Nightlife:
www.wallawalla.org
www.whitman.edu

Bars Close At:
Most close at 2:00 a.m. on weekends, though occasionally they'll stay open for special events.

Cheapest Place to Get a Drink:
Barnaby's

Local Specialties:
Any local Walla Walla wine, and anything that's not Keystone or Budweiser (the campus beers of choice)

Primary Areas with Nightlife
Main Street has a couple of places. There's a coffee shop that stays open late and often has live music, and Rosita's is right downtown. The Brew Pub's also close to campus, but doesn't have much atmosphere. Barnaby's and the Green Lantern are farther away, but worth the trip for some good dancing and drinking.

What to Do if You're Not 21
Rosita's often hosts eighteen and older gatherings, and although considered somewhat shady, the Underground also allows younger crowds to attend. Generally though, most students don't really need to leave campus for entertainment, especially those under twenty-one. Most often, the parties come to Whitman either in dorms, at house parties, or musical events. It is a rarity that there aren't at least a couple of options on any given weekend night.

Organization Parties
Whitman's drama crowd has been known to throw some pretty outrageous parties, especially cast parties where specialty drinks are readily available if you show up early.

House Parties
Whitman students are huge fans of house parties. Generally, houses with the better known nicknames establish reputations for great parties, and it's pretty much a given that most students will be there on a night when these are happening. It's also a great option for students when Greek functions are closed.

Frats
See the Greek Section!

Students Speak Out On...
Nightlife

> "Rosita's is pretty good for the younger crowds looking to get off campus. Barnaby's is the place that I've heard to be most popular, as well as the Green Lantern where they have really good music usually."

- "There are thee types of campus parties: **dorm parties, house parties, and frat parties.**"

- "I'm not too into the whole party scene, so **I don't pay much attention to the nightlife**. There are always music events going on, which is nice for those who don't necessarily want to drink. Most parties have alcohol, but you can avoid drinking if you really want to. I imagine the parties will mellow as I get older, or at least, I hope so."

- "Dorm parties generally entail **an excessive amount of drunk freshmen crammed into a tiny dorm room**, listening to blaring music and playing drinking games."

- "Students usually make the most effort to attend house parties, **since house parties allow for a bit more freedom**. These often have dancing and a bar or a keg, and people are generally expected to pitch in a few bucks for a keg cup to help out the party-throwers."

- "For the most part, frat parties, except for the beginning of the year ones, tend to be **solely for Greek members**."

- "Nightlife? **I usually watch movies and hang out with friends**. Occasionally, if it pleases me, I'll venture to the frats or a house party. But I don't mind that there's not a ton of nightlife—it would wear me out."

Q "**The Green Lantern is the main bar that people hang out at**. With cheap pitchers and a smoky ambiance, students often rendezvous in the evenings here."

Q "**Barnaby's is sketchy**, but the only place to dance at in Walla Walla, and the Brew Pub is next to campus, but is a bit more expensive."

Q "**Most of the nightlife happens on campus** unless you're older. For freshmen, it's frat parties and parties in their dorm rooms, for sophomores it's house parties and frat parties, for juniors, it's mainly house parties, and some off- campus bar hopping or clubbing, and for seniors, it's pretty much exclusively house parties, bars, and clubs."

The College Prowler Take On...
Nightlife

Since there isn't much to do in Walla Walla, in terms of clubs, bars, and concerts, most of these events take place on the Whitman campus. Nightlife primarily consists of campus parties (many of which are at the fraternities); concerts and musical events sponsored by Whitman. Almost every Friday night there's a musical event called "Coffeehouse," which takes place downstairs in Reid Campus Center—usually, students play there. There are also lecturers or speakers; screenings of movies sometimes shown on the big screen and dubbed "Drive-In Movies," and sometimes sporting events, specifically basketball games in the fall. Parties are the main source of amusement and entertainment on campus. Dorm parties are generally attended by first years, since it is first year students who live in the dorms (aside from the upper-classmen dorms like Douglass or North). Though the frats are generally pretty inviting, particularly for girls, they are most often exclusive if the party follows a Greek function. Other options for nightlife are the couple of bars and dance clubs directly off campus. Some students go to a club called "The Underground," although many Walla Walla police have dubbed it a sketchy, drug-ridden place, so many students tend to stay away from it. Other options include Barnaby's (a dance hall and bar), or the Brew Pub restaurant and bar. Some students (mostly those with cars) venture to the Tri-Cities to experience some of their dance clubs (both eighteen-and-up or twenty-one-and-up). Be prepared for some dull nights—particularly during the week, and occasionally on the weekends. All-in-all, most of the nightlife takes place on campus, and most students like the accessibility and openness of the parties and events there.

The College Prowler™ Grade on
Nightlife: C

A high grade in Nightlife indicates that there are many bars and clubs in the area that are easily accessible and affordable. Other determining factors include the number of options for the under-21 crowd and the prevalence of house parties.

Greek Life

The Lowdown On...
Greek Life

Number of Fraternities:
4

Number of Sororities:
4

Percent of Undergrad Men in Fraternities:
30-35%

Percent of Undergrad Women in Sororities:
30-35%

Fraternities on Campus:
Beta Theta Pi
Phi Delta Theta
Sigma Chi
Tau Kappa Epsilon

Sororities on Campus:
Delta Delta Delta
Delta Gamma
Kappa Alpha Theta
Kappa Kappa Gamma

Other Greek Organizations:
Greek Advisors
Interfraternity Council
Order of Omega
Pan Hellenic Council

Did You Know?

Contrary to many fraternities and sororities, Whitman's are very **active in community service** and sponsor annual events to raise money, ranging from "Most Beautiful Eyes" contest, to raising money for breast cancer organizations, to blood drives.

Students Speak Out On...
Greek Life

> "One of my favorite things about Whitman is how the Greek life happens alongside independent life. Granted, Greeks have a lot more organized social functions and periodically, as an independent, that was sometimes frustrating."

Q "It's pretty easy as a female to **take advantage of the frat parties** whenever I want to."

Q "It seems like it's harder as a guy to avoid Greek life. For some reason, as a girl, I feel like it's a bit easier to hang out with my sorority friends, Indy friends, and guy friends who are in the frats without feeling too much pressure. **Sometimes Greek life does stupid stuff**, like sponsoring dances with really off-color, offensive themes (like 'White Trash' dances or 'Old Men & School Girls'), but I manage not to get too fed up with it. I can't really complain because I take advantage of their parties too."

Q "It's great being in a frat. I've loved it, and the guys are all really awesome. I think if I hadn't joined, I wouldn't have seen my friends as much. The only major downfall is that **you have to live in the house**, and some parts of the TKE house are pretty crappy."

Q "**There's too many of them**—I do think it's a problem here at Whitman College especially since it's a small school it's very noticeable."

Q "It seems that **the majority of Greeks just hang out with each other and that's it**. Go to Prentiss (the dining hall) and see how many girls sit with just their Greek sisters!"

Q "**Greek life is a social scene unto itself**. Greeks tend to stick together, as do Indies."

Q "I think it is a much larger deal freshman year when **people are trying to find their place**, and its importance lessens each successive year."

Q "**I get fed up with all the Greek organizations on campus**, especially since we're a small school and it's very noticeable. But I do my best to avoid it, and although I dislike the larger group, most of the Greeks I know individually are really cool, nice people. I just don't like how exclusive their social group is."

Q "I've noticed that, as I've settled more into my own place at Whitman, Greek life becomes less and less prominent. It's a struggle as a freshman to figure out if it's really right for you, especially since Rush is really close to the beginning of the year, so you don't have much time to think about it. I have friends who are Greek, and most of them like it, but I do have some friends who wish they hadn't joined, and it's hard to de-pledge. I think, as an Indy, I have much more social freedom, which is nice. **I don't like people telling me how to dress and who to hang out with**!"

The College Prowler Take On...
Greek Life

The line dividing Greek life and independent life is pretty identifiable and rarely crosses over. Though all students are generally welcome to most Greek life events (and many attend when they are looking for a reliable and satisfying party), many of the Greek events are closed and force students in Greek life to only socialize with each other and get "sucked in and away" from other social events on campus. Some students like how this is set up. There is also the complaint of not liking the fashion in which the Greeks operate whether it be the themes of their parties or segregation amongst themselves, but students admit that the Greeks are good for social events.

Yes, it is frustrating to lose touch with friends who go Greek, or who stay independent, particularly because this does tend to set up how and with whom students socialize with for the duration of their time at Whitman. Overall, Greek life is annoying for the Independents and the Independents are, in essence, a group of whiners against the Greeks, making it very divided on campus. However, many students seem to find a happy balance without grudges, and though it's a bit more of a rarity, many students do manage to socialize with friends from both groups.

B

The College Prowler™ Grade on Greek Life: B

A high grade in Greek Life indicates that sororities and fraternities are not only present, but also active on campus. Other determining factors include the variety of houses available and the respect the Greek community receives from the rest of the campus.

Drug Scene

The Lowdown On...
Drug Scene

Most Prevalent Drugs on Campus:
Alcohol and marijuana

Drug Counseling Programs:
Drug counseling with the Counseling Center, one-on-one appointments available with Chuck Cleveland, Dean of Students

Liquor/Drug-Related Arrest

Unlike large universities, Whitman doesn't have a campus police department with the ability to make arrests. Any students who are arrested for drug or alcohol offenses would be arrested by the Walla Walla Police Department. So, Whitman doesn't have any kind of real data on such arrests. Anecdotally, it's really safe to say we have fewer problems than a larger university.

Students Speak Out On...
Drug Scene

"I've noticed that pot is being used more often, and it's easier to get, which is a little worrisome. Hopefully it won't become as popular as alcohol is on campus."

Q "The only prevalent drug on campus is pot (unless you count alcohol as a drug)."

Q "Alcohol seems to be the biggest form of substance abuse, and I don't think I can recall any weekend where it wasn't readily available at some party. **Whitman students definitely abuse alcohol** in my opinion, though I think the perception may be a bit more than it really is. It's at least nice to know that I don't have to worry about seeing anything much worse than alcohol on campus."

Q "Around finals, **some students abuse caffeine by taking pills or by fueling up on Red Bull** or coffee. Many pull all-nighters in the library, and I've caught wind a couple of times of people using speed, though this is a rarity and a rumor without much evidence. Beer seems to be the drug of choice, especially for guys who need a break in the library on late nights."

Q "**The school has a no-tolerance policy for marijuana**, though it's not uncommon for students who have it to be let off with warnings. If the Walla Walla police catch you, though, watch out—they're very unforgiving when it comes to drug use outside of underage drinking, and they really don't like busting up Whitman parties without whining about it."

Q "I really haven't heard of **anything 'harder' than pot** being used frequently."

Q "**I can't recall ever hearing of anything worse than alcohol or pot**, which is refreshing. If students did much more than that, it'd probably mess them up to the point where they couldn't do well academically, and since that's a large pressure here, most can't afford it unless there's something else going on with them that's more serious."

Q "I'd venture to say that illegal drugs are **not a problem** on campus."

Q "For a school that hosts **'The Beer Mile'**, it would seem like the obvious conclusion that alcohol is quite integrated into the lifestyle here. Though it can get out of control at times, most students don't drink so much that they get belligerent or pass out. For the few that do, the Health Center is really familiar with taking care of sick students, and at least one student ends up in the Health Center each weekend during the heavy party times."

Q "Drinking is probably **the most commonly used drug**, followed by pot."

The College Prowler Take On...
Drug Scene

As far as drugs are concerned at Whitman, the primary drug of choice is alcohol, and is in abundance. Although harder drugs do exist, they don't exist in a large enough way that they are noticed and highly problematic. Most students couldn't really respond to the drug scene because there isn't much of one. Although alcohol is very popular and probably the most abused substance on campus, drugs aside from marijuana are not seen regularly.

Yes, it is a rarity on the Whitman campus to attend a party where alcohol is not a major component to the atmosphere. However, many students would rather have alcohol in abundance than any other substance, particularly illegal drugs. Given that most substance abuse is centralized on alcohol, there is a certain pressure, of course, to drink—there is even an annual student-run tradition called "The Beer Mile". Whitman does have a well-deserved reputation for being a drinking school, but most students feel this is better than being known for pot or other illegal substance abuse. And, though it is sometimes a challenge on a Thursday or Friday night (Whitman's bigger party nights) to find a party without alcohol, it is even more challenging to find a party with illegal drugs. Overall, the drug scene and substance abuse are not extensive in variety or problematic for most students.

B

The College Prowler™ Grade on
Drug Scene: B

A high grade in the Drug Scene indicates that drugs are not a noticeable part of campus life; drug use is not visible, and no pressure to use them seems to exist.

Campus Strictness

The Lowdown On...
Campus Strictness

What Are You Most Likely to Get Caught Doing on Campus?
- Drinking underage
- Making too much noise in your dorm room
- Making too much noise anywhere on campus, especially if it's the weekend
- Having candles and incense in your dorm room
- Streaking or destroying public property
- Trying to sneak a keg into the dorms (they aren't allowed in dorm halls)
- Trying to sneak alcohol through dorm hallways
- Downloading copyrighted materials (especially music)
- Sneaking into the opposite sex's bathrooms
- Trying to swim in Lakum Duckum (a small pond where all the ducks in Walla Walla live)
- Smoking pot

Students Speak Out On...
Campus Strictness

"Whitman is somewhat strict. They're as strict as they need to be, at least, and I think they should be. It helps things run smoothly and reminds students that they are not invincible or able to escape deserved punishment."

Q "My Resident Director last year told me that **Whitman has the second most liberal, relaxed alcohol policy in the country**, second only to Reed College (in Oregon) that has no alcohol policy. It's great to be at a school that's this laid back, though at times I've seen policy enforced when it definitely needed to be."

Q "The campus is not especially [strict], although I have seen [campus policy] enforced, which it should be. **They are there to protect us and keep things semi-legal**. I've heard of people getting out of punishment after being caught with pot, so I imagine that they're not terribly strict about that [either]."

Q "Whitman's 'close door' policy is strict in the sense that **you're strongly discouraged from having alcohol out in public**, but at the same time, the enforcement varies so much from residence hall to residence hall that it is hard to call it strict, especially since there is no ban on drinking, only the location."

Q "**Drunkenness, on the other hand, is not regulated at all**. In my experience, the only trouble people ever got in was having lots of alcohol in public, and having to dump it out."

- "**Most students are pretty aware of their limits**, so Whitman doesn't need to be too strict to regulate them."

- "Since **there is such a strong focus on academics,** the administration isn't too strict about governing what students do to relieve some of the academic pressures."

- "Whitman really **only cracks down when things get dangerous** or risky for students, which rarely happens."

- "There are several systems in place to make sure things run smoothly. As an R.A., we went through extensive and rigorous training to learn about policy, and how to help those who are violating it. **These systems basically just ensure that students don't get hurt**, especially when their judgment is impaired, and they might not realize they're in potentially threatening situations."

- "**Students don't get too much flack from the administration**. They do their part when they're not partying, or violating policy, to make Whitman a good place."

- "**It depends on who catches you**. Security guards can sometimes be more lenient, and RAs are probably more likely to let you off with a warning if it's the first offense. But if it's the local police watch out. They're pretty brutal, and Whitman students have been known to suffer when caught by them."

The College Prowler Take On...
Campus Strictness

Technically, Whitman has a no-tolerance policy when it comes to drugs, but a very relaxed alcohol policy. In fact, first-year students are allowed to drink in their rooms as long as the door is shut and the group of people inside the room is small. Students, however, are not allowed to walk down the hall with an unsealed, open container of alcohol, but do not get in trouble necessarily for possessing alcohol.

Whitman's policies make the school a place that allows students enough room to experiment and have their fun with alcohol particularly. Whitman, in reality, is a pretty big drinking school, but it is very possible and common to find other social activities where alcohol is not involved. However, because of other factors (for example, how rigorous academics are), the relaxed policy lends itself to students governing their own lives and schedules. Those who spend too much time partying definitely end up paying for it academically or in some other way. Though generally, Whitman is a school that knows when to study hard and knows when to play hard. There are many options for students to have fun. Students looking for a non-exclusive party environment can find it very easily, and students who want to avoid the party scene can do so pretty easily as well.

B+

The College Prowler™ Grade on
Campus Strictness: B+

A high Campus Strictness grade implies an overall lenient atmosphere; police and RAs are fairly tolerant, and the administration's rules are flexible.

Parking

The Lowdown On...
Parking

Student Parking Lot?
Yes

Can Freshman Park?
Yes

Approximate Parking Permit Cost:
Free

Parking Permits:
None needed

Best Places to Find a Parking Spot:
Behind Harper Joy Theater, the Science building, Anderson Hall. RCC.

Good Luck Getting a Parking Spot Here:
Jewett Hall

Common Parking Tickets:
No Parking Zone: $40
Handicapped Zone: $200
Fire Lane: $100

Students Speak Out On...
Parking

> "I've definitely encountered difficulties when there are concerts or basketball games going on, and then it's really frustrating. I think if the school gets any bigger, they'll definitely need to expand their lots or build new ones."

Q "It can be frustrating to find parking when there is a big event going on, and **parking by the dorms is limited,** but not usually a major problem."

Q "**I've never known parking to be an issue**—most students don't need to drive that much unless they're going off campus. Jewett doesn't have much, but there seems to be enough parking on the street. The largest lots are farther away from the central parts of campus, so students mainly walk because they can take short cuts and get there faster."

Q "**The parking spaces at Prentiss are weird**! But [parking in general] is okay."

Q "Since most areas on campus are very accessible to each other, **it is really not necessary to drive anywhere on campus**, but if you do, I have never experienced any parking problems, except maybe on visitor's weekend."

Q "Depending on where you park, **there is a limited amount of parking space**, but it seems to be enough."

Q "I don't have a car, so **parking is not an issue for me**, which is nice. I haven't heard of it being a major problem, since we're a fairly small school, but friends of mine who do have cars have had trouble when big events are taking place or during Parent's Weekend."

Q "I imagine parking is more of a challenge for faculty, since **they have to share student parking**, and they come from off-campus, generally. Most of the students leave their cars in a parking spot for days, so they take some of the parking that the faculty could have."

Q "**Parking is fine**. It's free, which is the best part, and it's usually not hard to find a spot."

Q "I'm glad we're at a school that's small enough where **parking is not a problem**. I have friends at larger schools and universities who complain about it all the time, and are often late to class because they can't find a spot. That's never an issue here."

The College Prowler Take On...
Parking

For the most part, parking is not a major problem. Such a small school really doesn't seem to need much more than what it already has for parking, and most seem to think that the occasional overflow during big events isn't bad enough for more lots to be built. The dorms do have some parking, but most available parking is on the street, meaning students get pretty talented at parallel parking, although it's certainly possible to find parking in the lots unless large events are taking place. The occasional frustration arises when students need to find parking very close to their destinations, but there will always be some parking available nearby. Though most of the parking lots are fairly small, there are several of them, including lots by the science building, Olin, Jewett, Prentiss/Anderson, Reid Campus Center, Douglass, and at North. Students generally don't use their cars that often, unless it's for recreational purposes during the weekends, specifically for outdoor recreational activities since the surrounding terrain is known for its beauty and outdoor activities are very popular amongst Whitman students. It doesn't take too long for students to figure out where the best places to park are, and once students find these spots, they are pretty much guaranteed to be able to use the spot on a regular basis. Rarely, unless they are running very late to class and are desperate, do students use their cars to get to class (and if anyone found out, they'd probably be made fun of for the duration of the year). Overall, parking is almost always available on the street and it's free, which is a big bonus.

A-

The College Prowler™ Grade on Parking: A-

A high grade in this section indicates that parking is both available and affordable, and that parking enforcement isn't overly severe.

Transportation

The Lowdown On...
Transportation

Ways to get Around:
On Campus

Most students walk or ride their bikes. Occasionally students will skateboard, but the campus is small enough that any other transportation isn't necessary.

Taxi Cabs
A1 Taxi Cab
125 W. Alder Street
Walla Walla, WA 99362
(509) 529-2525

ABC Cabs
515 W. Pine Street
Walla Walla, WA 99362
(509) 529-7726

Public Transportation
Walla Walla has a pretty good bus system that goes to all the popular spots around town.

Local transit system:
Walla Walla City
200 S. 12th Avenue
Walla Walla, WA 99362
(509) 527-4429

Car Rentals

Alamo, local: (412) 472-5060; national: (800) 327-9633, www.alamo.com

Avis, local: (412) 472-5200; national: (800) 831-2847, www.avis.com

Budget, local: (412) 472-5252; national: (800) 527-0700, www.budget.com

Dollar, local: (412) 472-5100; national: (800) 800-4000. www.dollar.com

Enterprise, local: (412) 472-3490; national: (800) 736-8222, www.enterprise.com

Hertz, local: (412) 472-5955; national: (800) 654-3131, www.hertz.com

National, local: (412) 472-5094; national: (800) 227-7368, www.nationalcar.com

Best Ways to Get Around Town:

Walk. Everything you need is pretty much within walking distance.

Bum a ride from a friend, or nicely ask to borrow a car (Whitman students are nice enough that this happens pretty often.)

Ride a bike (students also let each other borrow bikes often)

Ways to Get Out of Town:

Airline Serving Walla Walla:

Horizon Air, affiliated with Alaska Air (800) ALASKAAIR (www.alaskaair.com)

Airport:

Walla Walla Airport

310 A Street

Walla Walla, WA 99362

(509) 525-3100

The Walla Walla Airport is approximately five or ten minutes driving time from campus, so it's a little over three or four miles away from Whitman.

Greyhound

Greyhound Bus Lines

315 N. 2nd Avenue

Walla Walla, WA 99362

(509) 525-9313

The Greyhound bus station is located approximately five minutes from campus near the highway on 2nd Avenue. For schedule information, call (509) 9313 or visit www.greyhound.com

Travel Agents

Carlson Wagonlit Travel
10 S. 4th Avenue
Walla Walla, WA 99362
(509) 525-0110

Cruise Planners
Walla Walla, WA 99362
(509) 525-8446

Jones Greg Jones International
10 S. 4th Avenue
Walla Walla, WA 99362
(509) 525-0110

Rainbow Cruises
Walla Walla, WA 99362
(509) 529-6952

Westwind Travel
513 N. Wilbur Avenue
Walla Walla, WA 99362
(509) 522-4847

World Wide Travel Service
11 S. 1st Avenue
Walla Walla, WA 99362
(509) 525-8040

Students Speak Out On...
Transportation

> "I don't know how often the locals use it, but I do know there's a bus system that goes to the busier parts of town. I've seen the main bus stop area before, but I have no idea where they drop off, and I've actually only seen public buses on a couple of rare occasions."

Q "There's public transportation?! I've **never used it!**"

Q "I'm not entirely sure [how convenient public transportation is], although I've heard from friends that **the trolley (or is it a bus?) is easily accessible**. I know there's a stop on campus. The town is so small that it doesn't really matter."

Q "There is a bus system, but I never had the occasion to use it—**many useful things are within walking distance**."

Q "There's a pretty cute touristy trolley that runs up and down Main Street. But aside from that, I assume there's a bus system, although I've never used it. Most everything I need is within walking distance or on campus, and in the event that I have to go farther, **I just get a ride from friends**."

Q "Public transportation is conveniently not necessary. **You can get anywhere on foot or bike**."

Q "Walla Walla is so small that **a public transportation system really isn't a necessity**, though they do have one. For Whitman students, it's certainly not used that often or even that well known. It doesn't really have to be since lots of people have cars, and are willing to give you rides if you need to go somewhere that isn't within a reasonable distance."

Q "Yeah there's a bus system. It's probably sufficient for Walla Walla, and Whitman kids don't seem to need it. **Most take taxis or get rides from people**, which seems like it's much easier to do anyway."

Q "**I didn't know Walla Walla had a bus system**! I wonder how good it is."

Q "You really don't need it—**you can walk everywhere** or ride a bike if you have one."

Q "I've heard of the Whitman vans being used more often than public transportation to get anywhere, actually. Whitman has at least **five huge vans that can seat eleven people each,** and it's not too hard to get certified to learn how to drive one. These seem to be more reliable than the Walla Walla public transportation system."

The College Prowler Take On...
Transportation

Since everything necessary is within walking distance, the public transportation system in Walla Walla is rarely used by students. Students who do need to get somewhere farther away either get rides from friends or borrow someone's car. Though the system is available, many students either are unaware of it or do not use it much if at all.

In fact, most students find the public transportation system unnecessary to use. Everything on campus is within walking distance, and many students bike; Safeway (the local grocery store) is also right down the street from campus; many restaurants are just on Main Street right down from campus as well, and the Greyhound bus station or Walla Walla airport are small, and close enough that students ask their friends with cars to drop them off or pick them up there. Overall, the public transportation system is extensive and adequate for such a small town, but on the up-side, since the town is so small, and most of what students need is right on campus (or not far away), it is not needed. If anything, borrowing students' cars, taking a taxi, getting rides from other students is more of Whitman's "public" transportation system, and students are always happy to help out.

The College Prowler™ Grade on Transportation: A-

A high grade for Transportation indicates that campus buses, public buses, cabs, and rental cars are readily-available and affordable. Other determining factors include proximity to an airport and the necessity of transportation.

Weather

The Lowdown On...
Weather

Average Temperature:
Fall: 53-79 °F
Winter: 29-41 °F
Spring: 37-72 °F
Summer: 54-90 °F

Average Precipitation:
Fall: 1.82 in.
Winter: 2.24 in.
Spring: 1.99 in.
Summer: 0.91 in.

Students Speak Out On...
Weather

> "Welcome to the land of 300 days of sunshine a year. Of course, the 65 days it isn't sunny are all in a row in January and February, and the fog never lifts, leaving everyone damp and cold."

Q "**The weather here is crazy**! Sometimes it can change very quickly."

Q "Winter is cold and in the summer it's hot. **It's nothing too out of the norm**."

Q "**The weather is usually sunny or overcast** but dry, especially when the year starts and ends. The beginning and end of the year are the best times weather wise—it's always sunny and really warm. Occasionally, it can get uncomfortably hot, but that's mainly in summer that this happens."

Q "Weather can get annoying in the late fall and winter because it tends to rain a lot or be overcast and gloomy. **Winters are tough because it gets really cold**, and I'm from California, so I'm not used to that. Fall semester seems to be better weather wise because it beats the long winter, and Spring semester starts off gray, cold, and dark, but with lots of sun and warmth at the end of the year. It seems to balance out."

Q "**Weather can get rough**. For those with Seasonal Disorder (sensitivity to seasonal changes and lack of sun), Whitman has a sun lamp that students are welcome to use that's free."

Q "**It can get windy, wet and (rarely!) snowy**. Winters are pretty dreary and overcast, so be prepared not to see the sun for a good long while."

Q "I'm from the Northwest, so the weather here is not too extreme. **It's usually sunnier here than it is in Western Washington**, and it doesn't seem to rain as much as in Oregon."

Q "Bring a variety of clothing, as it is humid and in the upper eighties in August and **it can get quite cold in the winter**."

Q "**Layers are key,** as is a fleece (because of its ability to keep out moisture)."

Q "**I like having an umbrella**, although most students don't use them."

Q "**It's always good to be prepared with a summer and winter wardrobe**, because you'll need both. I brought my pea coat, fleece, flannel PJs and sheets along with all my tank tops and shorts. I've worn all of them throughout the year for sure."

Q "Bring a wide array of clothes—**you'll want both the shorts/skirts and tank tops for early fall and spring**, but the warm sweaters come in handy when the fog just won't go away."

The College Prowler Take On...
Weather

Comparatively, Walla Walla's weather has been generally mild, but over the past few years, it has become a bit more intense. Last winter the snowstorms made it very difficult for students to get to campus before classes started (and once they did, the excessive snow on the ground made it difficult to do anything). Though occurrences such as these are a rarity, they have been known to happen, and Walla Walla's weather has been known to be fickle (one spring a couple of years ago it was eighty degrees one day, and the following day it snowed—go figure). Especially during later fall and into winter, Walla Walla can get quite foggy, too. Generally, Walla Walla definitely has seasonal changes, but on the milder side. But be prepared to feel the mood of the campus change with the weather—when it's rainy, overcast, and foggy, students aren't out and about as much, and so the campus feels quieter. But when it's sunny and warm out, it's nearly impossible to find students inside—most guys are topless with their shirts through their belt buckles, and the girls are in bathing suit tops with shorts or sarongs or skirts; everyone is barefoot; everyone is studying, reading or playing Frisbee on Ankeny field, and most are in a bubbly, zealous mood that's infectious, and inevitably affects the majority if not all students. Because of this, it gets pretty difficult to concentrate right around mid-late April until the remainder of the year. But Whitman students are pretty used to prioritizing academics, so most are able to conserve enough motivation to get their work done despite the distractions of the sunny, gorgeous weather.

B+

The College Prowler™ Grade on
Weather: B+

A high Weather grade designates that temperatures are mild and rarely reach extremes, that the campus tends to be sunny rather than rainy, and that weather is fairly consistent rather than unpredictable.

WHITMAN COLLEGE
Report Card Summary

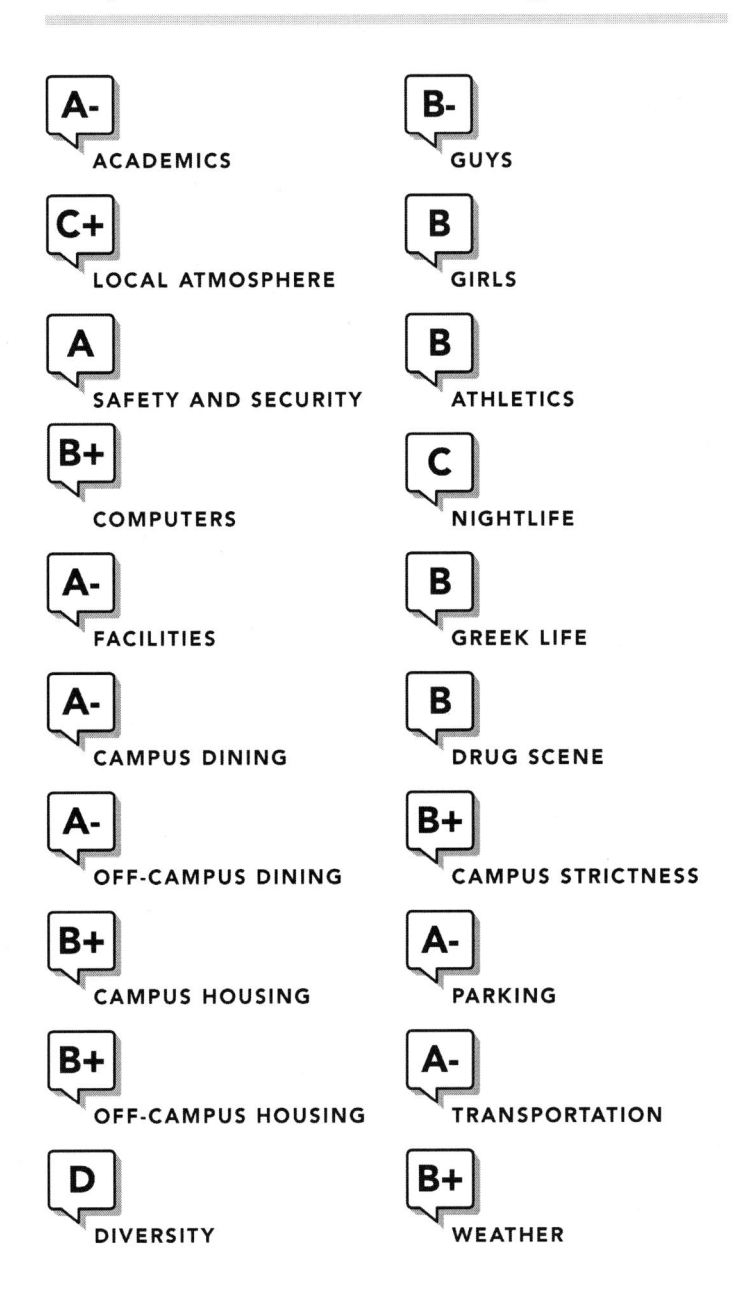

A- ACADEMICS

C+ LOCAL ATMOSPHERE

A SAFETY AND SECURITY

B+ COMPUTERS

A- FACILITIES

A- CAMPUS DINING

A- OFF-CAMPUS DINING

B+ CAMPUS HOUSING

B+ OFF-CAMPUS HOUSING

D DIVERSITY

B- GUYS

B GIRLS

B ATHLETICS

C NIGHTLIFE

B GREEK LIFE

B DRUG SCENE

B+ CAMPUS STRICTNESS

A- PARKING

A- TRANSPORTATION

B+ WEATHER

Overall Experience

Students Speak Out On...
Overall Experience

"Overall, my experience has been very educational and growthful; it has been rocky at times, but overall, very, very good. Sometimes I wish I were somewhere else, but when it comes down to it, I really love Whitman and appreciate it for what it is."

"Despite some of the poorer aspects, like the lack of diversity, I've loved my time at Whitman and think it's a phenomenal school. **I have had friends transfer, which is sad, but they always come back and visit** and one of them actually transferred back to Whitman. There are challenging aspects to adjust to like the weather, location and homogeny if they're different from what you're used to, but I can't imagine myself being happier anywhere else."

Q "Whitman has been everything I hoped it would be and much more. **I've always longed for the kind of close relationships I have with my professors**, and know they're always there to help, no matter what time of day or night. The professors genuinely love teaching, and dedicate their lifestyles to it—they're always welcome to give lectures at various events, and help students out with anything. I am so grateful to be in an environment that loves to learn and educate both in and out of the classroom."

Q "For a long time, I thought I wanted to transfer, actually. But after my first year, I came back and heard stories from friends about what their college experiences were like and realized that I have it pretty good out at Whitman. **The people are friendly and personable**, and though there are some social hurdles to jump over, everyone finds their place and feels comfortable eventually. My parents always tell me, after they meet my friends from Whitman, that they're impressed with how comfortable, well spoken, intelligent, and humorous they are. I'm proud to be a part of an environment where people are known to be these things."

Q "My freshman year was very difficult especially the diversity aspect of it—**it took a long time for me to find people I could identify with**. Students at Whitman are tired of hearing how Whitman is not diverse, but the problem with Whitman is that if they could make those few minority students [feel] that they belong to the Whitman community, to me, diversity would not be a problem. But the thing is, even those few working class students either end up leaving Whitman or just sucking it up—so that tells you that there's a problem. When I think about it, I do wish I'd transferred because then this aspect wouldn't have been so challenging. But, I know I'm a stronger person for staying and sticking it out."

Q "**My experience at Whitman improved each successive year I attended**. I loved Whitman and wish graduation hadn't come so soon."

Q "I've loved it. I'm graduating this year and **I'll be sad to leave.**"

Q "Never have I felt so comfortable in my surroundings. Of course, this was a hard adjustment to make, and it took some time, but **Whitman is a place where it's hard for people not to be themselves**, which is a great quality. I think, since the student body is accepting of peoples' eccentricities, weird hobbies, and quirks, the place creates an aura of comfort for people to just be. It's great not to have to worry about this when I'm trying to do well in classes, and just focus on furthering my academic education."

Q "If it weren't for all the remarkable people at this school, I doubt I'd still be here. But the great thing is that **professors and students alike are amazing** and always have something to contribute."

Q "**It seems like I just blinked and became a junior overnight.** That's how much fun it's all been."

Q "Whitman has been everything I longed for in high school. **There has been challenging class discussions**, a demanding and manageable course load, outgoing and friendly students who don't judge, and professors who care about who I am."

Q "I transferred here from a large university, and after being used to the luxuries of a larger school, that took a lot of adjusting. **It's frustrating that Whitman and Walla Walla don't offer the same things you can find at a bigger school**, or even a larger city, but people seem to manage okay, and I've learned how to adjust a bit. It's all worth it for the academics and the professors."

Q "The first few months were rough—getting used to such an open, liberal environment was challenging coming from my hometown and background, but **I wouldn't change the experience for anything**. I learned an equal amount from the living experiences and personal interactions at Whitman as I did in the classroom."

The College Prowler Take On...
Overall Experience

Though Whitman has had its ups and downs for most students overall, most have absolutely loved it and feel there is no possible college better for them. Many warn that it does take some getting used to (especially with Walla Walla being less metropolitan than what some are used to), but of course, that's a large part of what college itself is, no matter where you are. At Whitman, it's challenging to adjust to the environment if you find something drastically contrasting to what you're accustomed to before college, perhaps more so than it would be at other schools closer to larger cities. In general, most students have found they need to make some larger adjustment of some kind to Whitman's environment, but most have loved their experiences once they found a comfortable niche.

Many seniors find it difficult to leave Whitman because of the bonds they create with people there, be it with students or professors. Whitman also has a very strong and supportive network of alumni, which is indicative of the bond many people have with Whitman. Several students feel they've grown in many positive ways by being put through the challenges of Whitman, and all-in-all, wouldn't change their experiences there for the world. It's said to be a unique and special place unlike any environment most students have ever been in and many think it will be difficult to leave when graduation comes. The people really make the school, and are some of the most thoughtful, well-spoken, humorous, and genuine people you'll find anywhere.

The Inside Scoop

The Lowdown On...
The Inside Scoop

Whitman Slang:
Know the slang, know the school. The following is a list of things you really need to know before coming to Whitman. The more of these words you know, the better off you'll be.

ASH: acronym for the Asian Studies House

The Bakery: nickname of a party house down the streets from the frats

The Barn: nickname for the Delta Gamma party spot—it's actually a barn

Beer mile: an annual event created and sponsored by the cross country team where students run (often in the nude) a mile around Ankeny and have to chug a beer before each lap

CAB: acronym for Campus Activities Board, or the student-run campus planning committee that brings music, comedians, movies, and all sorts of fun events students want on campus

Carpet 2: nickname for a houseful of sorority sisters, located next to the carpet store, Carpet 1

Coffeehouse: often the name used when referring to the musical event on Friday nights, not the place itself

Duck Rape: the highly un-PC nickname used to describe duck mating season during late spring around campus

Eating a Beer: newfound trick in recent years where one shotguns a beer after biting into the can—brings a bit more entertainment to a stale drinking scene

FAH: acronym for the Fine Arts House (part of the IHC)

The Fishbowl: nickname for one of the better-known party houses in-between two of the frats

Frisbee Golf: reference to Whitman's very own Frisbee golf course set up throughout campus

GAH: acronym for the Global Awareness House (also IHC)

The Hospital: what some call North Hall, which used to be a hospital before Whitman turned it into a residence hall

IHC/IHM: the Interest House Community, recently nicknamed the Interest House Mafia

Indies: the nickname of non-affiliated students, those not in Greek Life

Inside Outhouse: nickname for the Outhouse (or environmental interest house)

La Casa: shortened name of La Casa Hispana, the Spanish House (IHC)

Lakum Duckum: name of the small pond next to the outdoor tennis courts where all the ducks in Walla Walla go—also sketchily infested with many forms of fungus or disease

Maxey Pad: nickname for Maxey Hall, the social science building

MECCA: acronym for the Multi-Ethnic Center for Cultural Awareness interest house

Mem: shortened name of the Memorial Building, where all of the main offices of the administration are

The Monstrosity: nickname of a huge white house down the street from RCC, notorious for huge parties

Mystical Intentions: recently created game that's a variation on volleyball, except players can only hold the volleyball when their feet aren't touching the ground.

Prospie: Whitman's popular nickname for prospective students, used with love

RCC: Reid Campus Center, or the student center

ResLife: shortened version of Residence Life

Sketchy: commonly used term by Whitman students to describe something strange or weird (also used by Walla Walla residents)

The SUB: the nickname students still use to refer to the former Student Union Building, recently replaced by Reid Campus Center

TC/TC Sightings: how students generally refer to the President, Tom Cronin, and his random appearances at various campus events

TEK: acronym for the Japanese interest house

Toss/ing the Disc: how many students refer to the act of playing Frisbee

Townie: what Whitman students call people from Walla Walla

Twittie: what Whitman students call people from Walla Walla who also happen to attend Whitman

WhitStock: big musical festival at the beginning of the year with all kinds of bands—local, campus, and from far and away

Whittie: nickname indicating how Whitman students refer to themselves and each other

Things I Wish I Knew Before Coming to Whitman

- Every student is a nerd…REALLY—though the school pretty much attracts nerds, so most people feel comfortable.
- Academic work is very demanding
- The frats and sororities have a strong presence on campus
- Winters are brutal and seem longer than they are
- Allergies are a big problem in spring and summer
- Rush if you're a guy (even if you don't intend to go Greek), skip most of it if you're a girl—guys go paint-balling, river rafting, and have BBQs, whereas the girls have tea parties
- Get on the cheapest meal plan possible
- Alcohol has a very strong presence
- The student body, racially, really isn't diverse
- Sign up for a rock climbing class early—they fill up fast
- Astronomy is a great class to take to meet science requirements in distribution

- Don't go to the library during finals unless you want to balance socializing with studying
- Walla Walla feels confining and small much of the time
- Tips to Succeed at Whitman:
- Have an open-mind about what you want to major in
- Take a wide variety of classes
- Form study groups with students from your classes and teach each other the course material as a method of studying—if you can teach the material, you know it
- Be open-minded socially—everyone has his or her quirky interests
- Get involved in student activities, but choose one or two activities to get involved in, so you don't encroach on your ability to perform well academically
- Either bring a car or have a good friend who has one, so you can periodically escape Walla Walla

Whitman Urban Legends

- The top floor of the library is the "best" place to hook-up
- Whitman can't have houses for sororities because Walla Walla law says they'd actually be brothels
- President Tom Cronin knows all the names of the boys, but has trouble remembering the girls' names
- Ghosts of former hospital patients still reside in North Hall
- One year, a female student who was so stressed out during finals week finally snapped and spent three days in a tree.

School Spirit

Though sporting events don't bring in an enormous amount of school spirit, every student I've talked to is very proud to be at Whitman. Students think very highly of the school, its professors, and all the resources it provides. The problem areas students hound Whitman for are predictable (lack of racial diversity, for instance), but generally, students are proud to be here. It's common for students to wear Whitman t-shirts or sweatshirts around campus, and almost inevitable that students start missing the school over breaks and after graduation, even after complaints during finals. In fact, many students have a hard time leaving Whitman because, somehow, the school just manages to charm its students, even with the fact that it's in Walla Walla.

Traditions

Whitstock - A musical festival taking place at the beginning of the year in fall with several bands, usually outdoors unless weather determines otherwise.

IHC Block Party - A block party sponsored by the Interest House Community, usually with several bands, a local Taco Truck for great Mexican, and booths set up from each house for activities.

Pinging - An experience all first-year students go through, kept highly secretive and enigmatic.

Beer Mile - A four-lap run around Ankeny field close to finals week where students run naked and drink beer (or beverages of choice) before each lap

Imagine Festival - Sponsored by the Multi-Cultural Center, this event promotes diversity and cultures of all kinds

Job Fair - Held by the Career Center to help set up jobs and internships with students and attended by several major companies in need of employees

Study Abroad Fair - Held by the Study Abroad Office to help students gather information about possible places they'd like to travel abroad, either during their time at Whitman or beyond

Duck Fest - Similar to "Pigs on Parade" in Seattle, this event showcases ducks made by Whitman students all throughout campus, later voted on, and the top winners receive money prizes

Bluemoon Release Party - The midnight release of Whitman's student run literary journal, the Bluemoon, accompanied by music and treats

Drag Fest - Recently a weeklong event celebrating all forms of sexuality with various events ending with a dance at the end of the week with professional drag queens, sponsored by Coalition Against Homophobia

Indy Choir Concert - A highly competitive event between independent choirs held in spring

Drive-In Movie Theater - Sponsored by CAB where movies (generally not yet available to rent) are shown on a huge screen next to Reid Campus Center on the lawn, free of charge

Onion Fest - Whitman's huge two to three day Ultimate Frisbee tournament with teams from the Northwest and beyond

Foam Party - One of the larger frat parties held annually at the beginning of the year with lots of sudsy foam

TKE Blood Drive - The annual blood drive held in the spring by the TKE fraternity

Finding a Job or Internship

The Lowdown On...
Finding a Job or Internship

Despite its smaller size, the Whitman Career Center has great connections with Whitman alumni and several other groups in need of students to help fill positions. The Career Center constantly emails students to keep them abreast of opportunities for work, and even has a library of helpful books, so students can research agencies that specialize in what they're interested in pursuing for summer work or after college.

Advice

Set up appointments with people in the Career Center—they are always very helpful, and go out of their way to help students. If you're looking for either an internship or a job, start early—they fill up fast and starting early allows you more time to go over options and see what other help the Career Center can provide if something falls through. Definitely attend the internship meetings and apply for both the Whitman Internship Fund and WA State Work Study Internship Fund if you qualify and find a great internship that doesn't pay well or at all. These funds allow you to get a certain amount of money from the state or Whitman in order to do your internship. Also, the Job Fair is a helpful and strategic event to network, and make connections at for future job prospects, so it's a good idea to attend that, as well.

Career Center Resources & Services:

Career Counseling
Placement Advising
Career Workshops
The Resource Center
Graduate School Advising
Career Center Job Announcements
Campus Employment

Average Salary Information

Although Whitman College does not officially track this information, the alumni office does confirm that many students continue into the medical field (particularly nursing) following graduation. Students participating in Whitman's pre-med and BBMB tracks often find success in the medical and science worlds. Other popular jobs after Whitman include jobs within law—in fact, many students from Whitman who pursue law school after their undergraduate degrees find they have a slight advantage when applying to many law schools. Though these career paths seem to be very popular amongst Whitman students after their undergraduate education, generally it is thought that most Whitman students do very well in any career they choose because of the fact that the school is so highly respected. Most people who hear a student has attended Whitman are very impressed and eager to hire a student with such a background.

Alumni

The Lowdown On...
Alumni

Website:
www.whitman.edu/alumni

Office:
Whitman College Alumni House
219 Marcus Street
Walla Walla, WA 99362
(509) 527-5167 or (800) 835-9448 ext. 1

Services Available:
Lifetime e-mail or snail mail newsletters and magazines
Guest room at Alumni House
Career Consultant Network
Annual Fund (Senior Fund), financial contributions to the college
Plans alumni events, both for current students to meet alumni, and also for reunions or other exclusively alumni events

Major Alumni Events:
Whitman College Campus Alumni Volunteer Leadership Conference
Whitman College Campus Fall Reunion Weekend
Whitman in Yellowstone
Whitman College Campus Spring Reunion
Whitman Alumni Baseball Games (attending games at SAFECO Baseball field in Seattle, WA), and other outdoor excursions.

Alumni Publications:
Whitman Magazine
E-mail newsletters

Famous Whitman Alumni:
- William O. Douglas '20 English-Economics, U.S. Supreme Court
- Ralph Cordiner '22 Economics-Political Science, CEO and Chairman, General Electric Corp.
- Walter Brattain '24 Physics, Physicist, Nobel Prize Winner
- Adam West' 51 English, Actor, "Batman"
- Matt Ames '70 Chemistry, Director of Research, Mayo Clinic
- Ryan Crocker '71 English, U.S. Ambassador to Afghanistan
- John Stanton '77 Political Science, Founder and CEO, Western Wireless & Voice Stream

Student Organizations

- Action For Animals : www.whitman.edu/afa
- American Indian Association : www.whitman.edu/aia
- Amnesty International : www.whitman.edu/amnesty_international
- Asian Cultural Association : www.whitman.edu/aca
- Associated Students of Whitman College: www.whitman.edu/aswc
- Ballroom Dancing : www.whitman.edu/ballroom
- Beta Theta Pi : www.whitman.edu/beta_theta_pi
- Bluemoon Journal : www.whitman.edu/bluemoon
- Coalition Against Homophobia : www.whitman.edu/cah
- Club Latino : www.whitman.edu/club_latino
- Cycling Club : www.whitman.edu/cycling
- Feminists Advocating Change and Empowerment : www.whitman.edu/face
- Fencing Club : www.whitman.edu/fencing
- GLBTQ : www.whitman.edu/glbtq
- Greek Life : www.whitman.edu/greek_life
- Whitman Ice Hockey : www.whitman.edu/ice_hockey
- The Whitman College Insurgency : www.whitman.edu/insurgency
- International Students and Friends Club : www.whitman.edu/international_club

- InterVarsity Christian Fellowship : www.whitman.edu/intervarsity
- Juggling Club : www.whitman.edu/jugglingclub
- KWCW 90.5 FM : www.whitman.edu/kwcw
- Lacrosse : www.whitman.edu/lacrosse
- L.E.A.D. : www.whitman.edu/lacrosse
- Organic Garden : www.whitman.edu/organic_garden
- Outdoor Program : www.whitman.edu/outdoor_program
- Peace Coalition : www.whitman.edu/peacecoalition
- Peer Listeners : www.whitman.edu/peer_listeners
- Phi Delta Theta : www.whitman.edu/phi_delta_theta
- Pioneer : www.whitman.edu/pioneer
- Renaissance Faire : www.whitman.edu/faire
- Republicans : www.whitman.edu/republicans
- Rugby : www.whitman.edu/rugby
- S.A.A.C.S. : www.whitman.edu/saacs
- Senior Fund : www.whitman.edu/senior_fund
- Shalom : www.whitman.edu/shalom
- Sigma Chi : www.whitman.edu/sigma_chi
- Sirens of Swank : www.whitman.edu/sirens
- Speech and Debate : www.whitman.edu/rhetoric/100forensics.htm
- Student Technology Advisory Committee : www.whitman.edu/stac
- Tae Kwon Do : www.whitman.edu/taekwondo
- Tau Kappa Epsilon : www.whitman.edu/tau_kappa_epsilon
- Testostertones : www.whitman.edu/testostertones
- Theatre Sports : www.whitman.edu/theatre_sports
- Ultimate Frisbee : www.whitman.edu/ultimate
- Whitman Civil Liberties Union : www.whitman.edu/wclu
- Whitman Investment Company : www.whitman.edu/wic
- Whitman Medieval Society : www.whitman.edu/wms
- Women in Science : www.whitman.edu/science_women
- Young Democrats : www.whitman.edu/democrats

The Best & The Worst

The Ten BEST Things About Whitman:

1. Friendliness of people
2. Accessibility of music and musical events
3. 24-hour, 7-day-week library
4. Professor accessibility and level of caring
5. Reading, socializing, or playing Frisbee on Ankeny field in the sun
6. Puns
7. Flex Dollars at Reid Café
8. Closet Nerds
9. Frisbee Golf
10. Humor on campus

The Ten **Worst** Things About Whitman:

1. Walla Walla
2. The State Penitentiary
3. Alcohol usage
4. Separation of Greek Life and Independents
5. Finals week
6. Harsh winter weather
7. Thin walls in Anderson, couch beds in Jewett, introverts in Lyman
8. Finding library computers at night or during finals
9. Stress and academic competition breeds on campus between students
10. Boy/Girl Ratio and the fact that many of the "good ones" are already taken

Visiting WC

The Lowdown On...
Visiting Whitman

Take a Campus Virtual Tour:
www.whitman.edu/tour/index.cfm

To Schedule a Group Information Session or Interview:
Call (509) 527-5176

Campus Tours and Overnight Visits:

Winter Schedule:
August 20 - May 19
Office Hours: 8:30 a.m. - 4:00 p.m., Weekdays
Campus Tours: 8:30-10, 11:00-12:15, 2:30-4:00 p.m.

Summer Schedule:
May 20 - August 19
Office Hours: 8:00 a.m. - 4:00 p.m., Weekdays

HOTEL INFORMATION

Best Western Walla Walla
7 East Oak
Walla Walla, WA
Phone: (509) 525-4700
Price: $65-$110
Web: www.bestwestern.com

Blue Mountain Motel
414 W. Main
Dayton, WA 99328
Phone: (509) 382-3040
Price: Starts at $40
Clean, well-kept rooms with updated amenities. Some kitchenettes available.

Budget Inn
305 North 2nd
Walla Walla, WA
Phone: (509) 529-4410
Price: $32-$70

Capri Motel
2003 Melrose
Walla Walla, WA 99362
Phone: (800) 451-1139
Price: $32.00 - $65.00

City Center Motel
627 West Main Street
Walla Walla, WA 99362
Phone: (509) 529- 2660
Prices: $38.50 - $185.00
Web: www.citycentermotelllc.com

Colonial Motel
2279 East Isaacs
Walla Walla, WA 99362
Phone: (509) 529-1220
Price: $45-$79
Web: www.colonial-motel.com

Dayton Motel
110 South Pine
Dayton, WA
Phone: (509) 382-4503
Price: $29-$65

Holiday Inn Express
1433 West Pine
Walla Walla, WA 99362
Phone: (509) 525-6200
Price: $59-$119
Web: www.holidayinnwallawalla.com

Howard Johnson Express Inn
325 East Main
Walla Walla, WA
Phone: (509) 529-4360
Price: $75-$159

La Quinta Inn
520 North Second Avenue
Walla Walla, WA 99362
Phone: (509) 525-2522
Price: $59-$149
Web: www.wallawallalaquinta.com

Marcus Whitman Hotel & Conference Center
Six West Rose Street
Walla Walla, WA 99362
Phone: (509) 525-2200
Price: Moderate
Web: www.marcuswhitmanhotel.com

Morgan Inn
104 N. Columbia
Milton-Freewater, WA
Phone: (541) 938-5547
Price: $42.75-$105

Out West Motel
84040 Highway 11
Milton-Freewater, WA
Phone: (541) 938-6647
Price: $42-$55

Super 8 Motel
2315 Eastgate St N
Walla Walla, WA 99362
Phone: (509) 525-8800
Price: $49 to $104
Web: www.super8.com

Travelodge
421 East Main
Walla Walla, WA
Phone: (509) 529-4940
Price: $44-$77
Web: www.travellodge.com

Walla Walla Residential Suites
214 East Main
Walla Walla, WA
Phone: (509) 525-7322
Price: $75-$95

Weinhard Hotel
235 E. Main Street
Dayton, WA 99328
Phone: (509) 382-4032
Price: Starts at $90
Web: www.weinhard.com

DIRECTIONS TO CAMPUS
Driving from the North:
- Merge onto I-90 W/US-2 W/US-395 S.
- Merge onto US-195 S via exit number 279 toward COLFAX/PULLMAN.
- Stay straight to go onto W WALLA WALLA HWY/WA-26. Continue to follow WA-26.
- Turn LEFT onto WA-127.
- WA-127 becomes US-12.
- Turn LEFT onto COPPEI AVE/US-12. Continue to follow US-12 W.
- Turn LEFT onto CLINTON ST.
- Turn RIGHT onto BOYER AVE.
- End at 345 BOYER AVE WALLA WALLA WA

Driving from the South:
- Merge onto I-80 E
- Merge onto I-505 N
- I-505 N becomes I-5 N.
- Merge onto I-205 N/VETERANS MEMORIAL HWY via exit number 288 toward I-84/THE DALLES/SEATTLE.
- Merge onto I-84 E via exit number 22 toward THE DALLES/MT. HOOD/COLUMBIA RIVER GORGE.
- Take the OR-11 exit- exit number 210- toward PENDLETON/MILTON - FREEWATER.
- Turn LEFT onto OREGON WASHINGTON HWY/OR-11.
- Turn RIGHT onto SE COURT AVE/OR-11/OREGON WASHINGTON HWY. Continue to follow SE COURT AVE.
- Turn SLIGHT LEFT onto OREGON WASHINGTON HWY/OR-11.
- OREGON WASHINGTON HWY/OR-11 becomes WA-125 N.
- Turn RIGHT onto W POPLAR ST.
- Turn SLIGHT RIGHT onto ALDER ST.
- Turn LEFT onto S PARK ST.
- Turn RIGHT onto BOYER AVE.
- End at 345 BOYER AVE WALLA WALLA WA

Driving from the East:

- Take W FRONT ST/US-20 W/US-26 W. Continue to follow US-20 W/US-26 W
- Stay straight to go onto I-184 W.
- Merge onto I-84 W via the exit- on the left.
- Merge onto PENDLETON HWY/US-30 via exit number 213 toward PENDLETON CITY CTR./NATIONAL HISTORIC DISTRICT.
- Turn SLIGHT RIGHT.
- Turn RIGHT onto OREGON WASHINGTON HWY/OR-11.
- OREGON WASHINGTON HWY/OR-11 becomes WA-125 N.
- Turn RIGHT onto W POPLAR ST.
- Turn SLIGHT RIGHT onto ALDER ST.
- Turn LEFT onto S PARK ST.
- Turn RIGHT onto BOYER AVE.
- End at 345 BOYER AVE WALLA WALLA WA

Driving from the West:

- Take I-5/I-90 E ramp toward PORTLAND.
- Merge onto I-90 E via the exit- on the left- toward BELLEVUE/SPOKANE.
- Merge onto I-82 E via exit number 110 toward YAKIMA.
- Merge onto US-12 E via exit number 102 toward RICHLAND/PASCO.
- Take the 2ND AVE. exit toward CITY CENTER.
- Turn LEFT onto N 2ND AVE/US-12 BR.
- Turn LEFT onto E ROSE ST.
- Turn RIGHT onto N PALOUSE ST.
- Turn SLIGHT LEFT onto BOYER AVE.
- End at 345 BOYER AVE WALLA WALLA WA

Words to Know

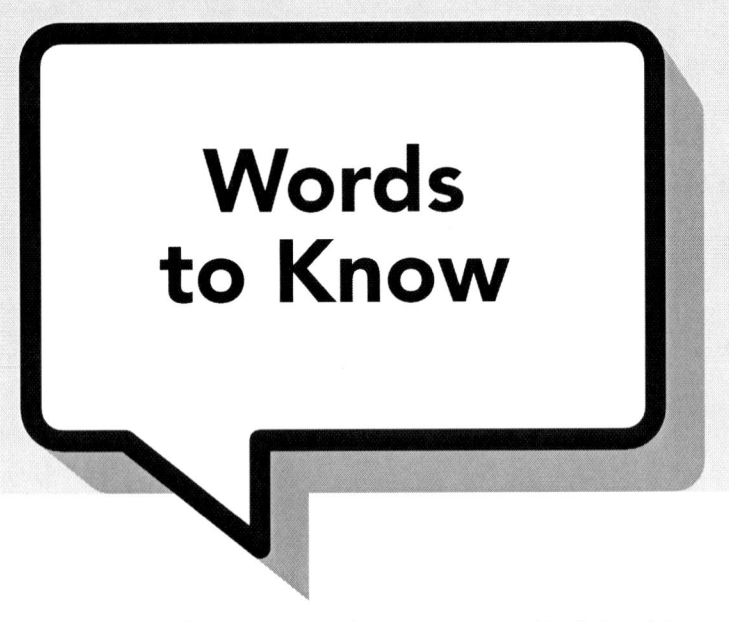

Academic Probation – A student can receive this if they fail to keep up with their school's academic minimums. Those who are unable to improve their grades after receiving this warning can possibly face dismissal.

Beer Pong / Beirut – A drinking game with numerous cups of beer arranged in a particular pattern on each side of a table. The goal is to get a ping pong ball into one of the opponent's cups by throwing the ball or hitting it with a paddle. If the ball lands in a cup, the opponent is required to drink the beer.

Bid – An invitation from a fraternity or sorority to pledge their specific house.

Blue-Light Phone – Brightly-colored phone posts with a blue light bulb on top. These phones exist for security purposes and are located at various outside locations around most campuses. If a student has an emergency or is feeling endangered, they can pick up one of these phones (free of charge) to connect with campus police or an escort service.

Campus Police – Policemen who are specifically assigned to a given institution. Campus police are not regular city officers; they are employed by the university in a full-time capacity.

Club Sports – A level of sports that falls somewhere between varsity and intramural. If a student is unable to commit to a varsity team but has a lot of passion for athletics, a club sport could be a better, less intense option. If a club sport still requires too much commitment, intramurals often involve no traveling and a lot less time.

Cocaine – An illegal drug. Also known as "coke" or "blow," cocaine often resembles a white crystalline or powdery substance. It is highly addictive and dangerous.

Common Application – An application that students can use to apply to multiple schools.

Course Registration – The time when a student selects what courses they would like for the upcoming quarter or semester. Prior to registration, it is best to have an idea of several back-up courses in case a particular class becomes full. If a course is full, a student can place themselves on the waitlist, although this still does not guarantee entry.

Division Athletics – Athletics range from Division I to Division III. Division IA is the most competitive, while Division III is considered to be the least competitive.

Dorm – Short for dormitory, a dorm is an on-campus housing facility. Dorms can provide a range of options from suite-style rooms to more communal options that include shared bathrooms. Most first-year students live in dorms. Some upperclassmen who wish to stay on campus also choose this option.

Early Action – A way to apply to a school and get an early acceptance response without a binding commitment. This is a system that is becoming less and less available.

Early Decision – An option that students should use only if they are positive that a place is their dream school. If a student applies to a school using the early decision option and is admitted, they are required and bound to attend that university. Admission rates are usually higher with early decision students because the school knows that a student is making them their first choice.

Ecstasy – An illegal drug. Also known as "E" or "X," ecstasy looks like a pill and most resembles an aspirin. Considered a party drug, ecstasy is very dangerous and can be deadly.

Ethernet – An extremely fast internet connection that is usually available in most university-owned residence halls. To use an Ethernet connection properly, a student will need a network card and cable for their computer.

Fake ID – A counterfeit identification card that contains false information. Most commonly, students get fake IDs and change their birthdates so that they appear to be older than 21 (of legal drinking age). Even though it is illegal, many college students have fake IDs in hopes of purchasing alcohol or getting into bars.

Frosh – Slang for "freshmen."

Hazing – Initiation rituals that must be completed for membership into some fraternities or sororities. Numerous universities have outlawed hazing due to its degrading or dangerous requirements.

Sports (IMs) – A popular, and usually free, student activity where students create teams and compete against other groups for fun. These sports vary in competitiveness and can include a range of activities—everything from billiards to water polo. IM sports are a great way to meet people with similar interests.

Keg – Officially called a half barrel, a keg contains roughly 200 12-ounce servings of beer and is often found at college parties.

LSD – An illegal drug. Also known as acid, this hallucinogenic drug most commonly resembles a tab of paper.

Marijuana – An illegal drug. Also known as weed or pot; besides alcohol, marijuana is one of the most commonly-found drugs on campuses across the country.

Major – The focal point of a student's college studies; a specific topic that is studied for a degree. Examples of majors include physics, English, history, computer science, economics, business, and music. Many students decide on a specific major before arriving on campus, while others are simply "undecided" and figure it out later. Those who are extremely interested in two areas can also choose to double major.

Meal Block – The equivalent of one meal. Students on a "meal plan" usually receive a fixed number of meals per week.

Each meal, or "block," can be redeemed at the school's dining facilities in place of cash. More often than not, if a student fails to use their weekly allotment of meal blocks, they will be forfeited.

Minor – An additional focal point in a student's education. Often serving as a compliment or addition to a student's main area of focus, a minor has fewer requirements and prerequisites to fulfill than a major. Minors are not required for graduation from most schools; however some students who want to further explore many different interests choose to have both a major and a minor.

Mushrooms – An illegal drug. Also known as "shrooms," this drug looks like regular mushrooms but are extremely hallucinogenic.

Off-Campus Housing – Housing from a particular landlord or rental group that is not affiliated with the university. Depending on the college, off-campus housing can range from extremely popular to non-existent. Those students who choose to live off campus are typically given more freedom, but they also have to deal with things such as possible subletting scenarios, furniture, and bills. In addition to these factors, rental prices and distance often affect a student's decision to move off campus.

Office Hours – Time that teachers set aside for students who have questions about the coursework. Office hours are a good place for students to go over any problems and to show interest in the subject material.

Pledging – The time after a student has gone through rush, received a bid, and has chosen a particular fraternity or sorority they would like to join. Pledging usually lasts anywhere from one to two semesters. Once the pledging period is complete and a particular student has done everything that is required to become a member, they are considered a brother or sister. If a fraternity or a sorority would decide to "haze" a group of students, these initiation rituals would take place during the pledging period.

Private Institution – A school that does not use taxpayers dollars to help subsidize education costs. Private schools typically cost more than public schools and are usually smaller.

Prof – Slang for "professor."

Public Institution – A school that uses taxpayers dollars to help subsidize education costs. Public schools are often a good value for in-state residents and tend to be larger than most private colleges.

Quarter System (sometimes referred to as the Trimester System) – A type of academic calendar system. In this setup, students take classes for three academic periods. The first quarter usually starts in late September or early October and concludes right before Christmas. The second quarter usually starts around early to mid–January and finishes up around March or April. The last quarter, or "third quarter," usually starts in late March or early April and finishes up in late May or Mid-June. The fourth quarter is summer. The major difference between the quarter system and semester system is that students take more courses but with less coverage.

RA (Resident Assistant) – A student leader who is assigned to a particular floor in a dormitory in order to help to the other students who live there. A RA's duties include ensuring student safety and providing guidance or assistance wherever possible.

Recitation – An extension of a specific course; a "review" session of sorts. Because some classes are so large, recitations offer a setting with fewer students where students can ask questions and get help from professors or TAs in a more personalized environment. As a result, it is common for most large lecture classes to be supplemented with recitations.

Rolling Admissions – A form of admissions. Most commonly found at public institutions, schools with this type of policy continue to accept students throughout the year until their class sizes are met. For example, some schools begin accepting students as early as December and will continue to do so until April or May.

Room and Board – This is typically the combined cost of a university-owned room and a meal plan.

Room Draw/Housing Lottery – A common way to pick on-campus room assignments for the following year. If a student decides to remain in university-owned housing, they are assigned a unique number that, along with seniority, is used to choose their new rooms for the next year.

Rush – The period in which students can meet the brothers and sisters of a particular chapter and find out if a given fraternity or sorority is right for them. Rushing a fraternity or a sorority is not a requirement at any school. The goal of rush is to give students who are serious about pledging a feel for what to expect.

Semester System – The most common type of academic calendar system at college campuses. This setup typically includes two semesters in a given school year. The "fall" semester starts around the end of August or early September and finishes right before winter vacation. The "spring" semester usually starts in mid-January and ends around late April or May.

Student Center/Rec Center/Student Union – A common area on campus that often contains study areas, recreation facilities, and eateries. This building is often a good place to meet up with fellow students and is most commonly used as a hangout. Depending on the school, the student center can have a huge role or a non-existent role in campus life.

Student ID – A university-issued photo ID that serves as a student's key to many different functions within an institution. Some schools require students to show these cards in order to get into dorms, libraries, cafeterias, and other facilities. In addition to storing meal plan information, in some cases, a student ID can actually work as a debit card and allow students to purchase things from bookstores or local shops.

Suite – A type of dorm room. Unlike other places that have communal bathrooms that are shared by the entire floor, a suite has a private bathroom. Suite-style dorm rooms can house anywhere from two to ten students.

TA (Teacher's Assistant) – An undergraduate or grad student who helps in some manner with a specific course. In some cases, a TA will teach a class, assist a professor, grade assignments, or conduct office hours.

Undergraduate – A student who is in the process of studying for their Bachelor (college) degree.

ABOUT THE AUTHOR:

Writing this book was not only a great way for me to indulge my passion for writing, but to realize what an amazing place Whitman has been for me. If it hadn't been for the Whitman Career Center forwarding me the e-mail about this opportunity, you might not be reading my words. Hopefully, this rare opportunity will help open some doors, but all I can do for now is cross my fingers, and be hopeful as I finish up the last two years of my time at Whitman.

In no particular order I give the following all my sincerest, warmest, and most heartfelt thanks for contributing to me and my life, and this end product, as well, for without them, what's on these pages would not have been possible: Mom, Dad, Jamie (a.k.a. Hi-Mee)—thanks for your unconditional love and support in all its forms, for that I am eternally grateful, and always proud to seek that which is unusual, humorous, unique, eccentric and everything else beyond what's normal; the greatest friends in the world from Bainbridge (I love you all!), Betsy, Erica, Wendy, Steve, Alice, John, Kara, Marty, Mike & family, the jump rope girls and all of you who I may have missed, though you all know who you are—you all embody what I know to be perfect, remarkable, and extraordinary in this world and my life would not be complete without each and every one of you in it; my newfound soul mates at Whitman, Rachel (the most understanding and thoughtful human being I know—I love you more than I can say), Drew (perhaps the funniest and most talented human being I know—I love you too, of course), the Residence Life Staff—you've all seen me at my best and at my worst, yet you still love me, offer me support, and ears to listen, and for that, you have made my time at Whitman a time I'll treasure for the rest of my life; my professors at Whitman—Hashimoto, Michelle Janning, Nanette Thrush, Betty McCall who never fails to inspire, humor, guide, and impassion me even in the most stressful of times; David Layton who always taught me to seek greatness and enjoy the wonderful plainness of life; Bob McAllister who taught me that genius lies in detail, to embrace your madness, and let all the good and the bad come out in written form; and finally, to all of the outstanding people at College Prowler, for having faith in me to write this book and for helping me take one step closer to my dreams.

Carly N. Sanders, Author
Carlysanders@collegeprowler.com

Notes

Notes

Notes

Notes

Notes

Notes

Notes

Notes

Notes

Notes

Notes

Notes

Notes

Notes

Notes

Notes

Notes

Notes

Need More Help?

Do you have more questions about this school? Can't find a certain statistic? College Prowler is here to help. We are the best source of college information on the planet. We have a network of thousands of students who can get the latest information on any school to you ASAP. E-mail us at *info@collegeprowler.com* with your college-related questions. It's like having an older sibling show you the ropes!

Email Us Your College-Related Questions!

Check out **www.collegeprowler.com** for more details.
1.800.290.2682

Notes

Tell Us What Life Is Really Like At Your School!

Have you ever wanted to let people know what your school is really like? Now's your chance to help millions of high school students choose the right school.

Let your voice be heard and win cash and prizes!

Check out **www.collegeprowler.com** for more info!

COLLEGE PROWLER™

Notes

Do You Have What It Takes To Get Admitted?

The College Prowler Road to College Counseling Program is here. An admissions officer will review your candidacy at the school of your choice and create a 12+ page personal admission plan. We rate your credentials with the same criteria used by school admissions committees. We assess your strengths and weaknesses and create a plan of action that makes a difference.

Check out **www.collegeprowler.com** or call 1.800.290.2682 for complete details.

COLLEGE PROWLER™

Notes

Pros and Cons

Still can't figure out if this is the right school for you? You've already read through this in-depth guide; why not list the pros and cons? It will really help with narrowing down your decision and determining whether or not this school is right for you.

Pros	Cons

COLLEGE PROWLER

Notes

Need Help Paying For School?
Apply for our Scholarship!

College Prowler awards thousands of dollars a year to students who compose the best essays. E-mail *scholarship@collegeprowler.com* for more information, or call 1.800.290.2682.

Apply now at **www.collegeprowler.com**

COLLEGE PROWLER™

Notes

Get Paid To Rep Your City!

Make money for college!

Earn cash by telling your friends about College Prowler!

Excellent Pay + Incentives + Bonuses

Compete with reps across the nation for cash bonuses

Gain marketing and communication skills

Build your resume and gain work experience for future career opportunities

Flexible work hours; make your own schedule

Opportunities for advancement

Contact *sales@collegeprowler.com*
Apply now at **www.collegeprowler.com**

COLLEGE PROWLER™

Notes

Do You Own A Website?

Would you like to be an affiliate of one of the fastest-growing companies in the publishing industry? Our web affiliates generate a significant income based on customers whom they refer to our website. Start making some cash now! Contact *sales@collegeprowler.com* for more information or call 1.800.290.2682

Apply now at **www.collegeprowler.com**

COLLEGE PROWLER™

Notes

Reach A Market Of Over 24 Million People.

Advertising with College Prowler will provide you with an environment in which your message will be read and respected. Place your message in a College Prowler guidebook, and let us start bringing long-lasting customers to you. We deliver high-quality ads in color or black-and-white throughout our guidebooks.

Contact Joey Rahimi
joey@collegeprowler.com
412.697.1391
1.800.290.2682

Check out **www.collegeprowler.com** for more info.

COLLEGE PROWLER™

Notes

Write For Us!
Get Published! Voice Your Opinion.

Writing a College Prowler guidebook is both fun and rewarding; our open-ended format allows your own creativity free reign. Our writers have been featured in national newspapers and have seen their names in bookstores across the country. Now is your chance to break into the publishing industry with one of the country's fastest-growing publishers!

Apply now at **www.collegeprowler.com**

Contact *editor@collegeprowler.com* or call 1.800.290.2682 for more details.

Notes

Notes

Notes

Notes

Notes

Notes

Notes

Notes

Notes